THIS ANCIENT HEART

I found this book delightful. It brings us to old, ancient doors that have been waiting for us to open them for maybe millennia. With perspectives from liminal threshold women and men including Emma Restall Orr, Caitlin Matthews, Jenny Blain, Greywolf and Robert Wallis, who have lived and worked with our native traditions for most of their lives, there is a wealth of experience and wisdom here. A book to dip into for years to come.

Elen Sentier, author of *The Celtic Chakras, Elen of the Ways* and *Trees of the Goddess*

Most Pagans look to the past for inspiration. How we relate to our ancestors, who we even understand them to be, and what we carry, real or imagined, into the future is often a key question for modern Pagans. This book offers an intriguing array of insights, ideas, challenges and possibilities that help the reader consider their own relationship with issues of ancestry, identity and belonging.

Nimue Brown, author of *Druidry and the Ancestors*

This volume is an absolute treasure trove – a stunning collection of essays that offer much food for thought for every spiritual seeker.

Philip Carr Gomm, Chief of Order of Bards, Ovates and Druids, Psychologist and author of *Druid Mysteries and Sacred Places*, and co-author a number of books including *The Book of English Magic* (with Richard Heygate) and *The DruidCraft Tarot* (with Stephanie Carr-Gomm)

This Ancient Heart perfectly expresses why I became a Pagan Druid in the first place; not as an act of rebellion against some church or any particular God, but because I fell deeply and irrevocably in love with our ancient common ancestress; Great Nature, 'The Mother of Ten Thousand Things'. These words invite us to remember our place in the universe, and to experience ecstatic reunion with All That Is; I am Goddess and You are God and so is every rock, seed, tree, bird, insect, river, fish, mountain, four legged and two legged in this sacred creation we inhabit. Holding to that awareness we may perhaps yet preserve a future for the Earth and her creatures.

Ellen Evert Hopman, author of *A Legacy of Druids* (Moon Books) and *A Druids Herbal of Sacred Tree Medicine* (Destiny Books)

What does the progress of humankind, the development of knowledge, technology and modern science mean when we lose the connection between our Soul, the All-Being and the Ancestors?

To restore the quiet dialogue with the Ancestors is the ultimate challenge of the authors of this book.

These chapters invite you, the reader, to follow in the footsteps of the authors and visit ancient sites and to find out, for yourself as a pilgrim, what these sites mean to you.

Beyond our power to think, we find a sea of imagination that open doorways to the unexpected, the curious and the fascinating. This place feels like a dream that is full of truths. Open this doorway and let your imagination flow and the chapters within this book become a magical stream of letters that dance together in a timeless, secret message.

Osarkak, a storyteller of Greenland, says: 'All our sagas are experiences of men. They are true. What our wise ancestors passed on are no lies or rash phrases. If people of our time think that a lot of these episodes are not true it means that only their lifeforces are thinner than those of the Ancestors from whom we derive it'.

The authors let no one stand before a closed door, so take the challenge, read the book, pass the doorway, the gateway and go on your quest, your pilgrimage.

Chantal Hoyberghs, historian and Druid

This Ancient Heart

The Threefold Relationship
Between Landscape, Ancestor
and Self

This Ancient Heart

The Threefold Relationship
Between Landscape, Ancestor
and Self

Paul Davies and Caitlín Matthews

(editors)

MOON
BOOKS

Winchester, UK
Washington, USA

First published by Moon Books, 2015
Moon Books is an imprint of John Hunt Publishing Ltd., Laurel House, Station Approach,
Alresford, Hants, SO24 9JH, UK
office1@jhpbooks.net
www.johnhuntpublishing.com
www.moon-books.net

For distributor details and how to order please visit the 'Ordering' section on our website.

Text copyright: Paul Davies and Caitlín Matthews 2014

ISBN: 978 1 78279 967 2
Library of Congress Control Number: 2015936387

A CIP catalogue record for this book is available from the British Library.

Design: Stuart Davies

Printed and bound by CPI Group (UK) Ltd, Croydon, CR0 4YY, UK

We operate a distinctive and ethical publishing philosophy in all
areas of our business, from our global network of authors to
production and worldwide distribution.

CONTENTS

For Tim Sebastian, SOD.

Foreword

By Graham Harvey

Something curious is emerging from the heart of the modern world; something not only unexpected, but perhaps the opposite of what was expected. This something is not a simple thing, and not a small thing. It is a complex assemblage that requires more than a quick glance to get what is happening. Nonetheless, for this foreword I'll offer a brief scan of matters that I find significant as a scholar of religion (for more, see Harvey 2013).

Much of the curious, unexpected and fascinating is revealed in the book you are now reading. That is, part of what was not supposed to happen in the modern world has to do with ancestors. Once, but not so long ago, it might have been enough for people writing about ancestors to say what the word means to people unlike ourselves. Indigenous peoples far away could be said to hold the peculiar notion that dead people mattered. Or maybe ancient people here at the heart of empire could be called 'ancestors' to distinguish them from the recently deceased. There are other ways of thinking about the word 'ancestor', but we need not elaborate on them now. It is likely that anyone who has read what this book is about (perhaps by reading the cover blurb or advertising copy) will have had thoughts about the meanings of the word. It is, as with any book, important that readers begin with some reflections about their own expectations and anticipations. In the hope that you have already done that, I want to say why I think that the interest in ancestors shared by authors and readers of this book (and by those to whom we might recommend this book) is a curious and unexpected thing.

The idea that ancestors could be of interest to the living, and the idea that the living could still be of interest to those who have died, could once have been labelled 'primitive', because these were ideas that were supposed to have been abandoned. Indeed, although it might seem that progress into modernity involved simply dropping or forgetting any idea of ongoing relationships between the living and the dead, in truth ancestors were actively rejected. Well, of course, no-one who puts flowers on a grave or memorial, no-one who celebrates a historic anniversary, and no-one who wishes their heritage to be more highly valued, has really rejected ancestors. Nonetheless, few people, even of those who do put flowers on graves and so on, live their lives as if those who have died are entirely present *now* in any meaningful, everyday sense. Typically in contemporary English, 'ancestors' means 'long gone and almost forgotten'. Often we think of ancestors as those dead people whose names we have forgotten. They are a largely anonymous crowd. Having handed on life to their children and children's children, and hence to us, they and their deeds and desires begin to fade out of living memory or daily relevance. Perhaps they become part of the background – just as these thoughts of mine are part of the background of the book. Abandoning or forgetting ancestors seems an unsurprising aspect of the long flow of history, one thing after another, one person or generation after another, with remoteness feeding vagueness.

However, to seek to remember those ancestral generations is not the curious thing. There is nothing radical about noting that we are not the first humans. It is hardly even unusual to celebrate the achievements of those who built amazing structures (to nod politely to the punch-line of *The Epic of Gilgamesh* – which might be paraphrased as: only the walls kings build will survive their inevitable deaths, and lesser mortals will have lesser memorials and fade from memory faster). What is curious is that modern people are once again seeking to honour ancestors in ways that seem to matter to them. This book will offer more than a few engagements with such varied and sometimes colourful efforts. There are wonderfully imaginative approaches to consider. Some you may never have thought of; some may change your journey through the world. It may be hard to fuse all that is presented here into one simple thought or practice. Indeed, I hope that it will be impossible to reduce what is ahead into one definitive statement to which all the authors, let alone all the readers, will assent. This, too, however, is not unexpected.

My claim that something curious is happening in the world, and that this unexpected and even unwanted thing has something to do with ancestors, is in part inspired by a bigger surprise. The anthropologist of religion Robert Orsi has written that, 'The modern world was not supposed to look the way it does.' (Orsi 2012: 146) He was not writing about the renewal of ancestor veneration or even of the acknowledgement of the presence of the deceased in contemporary lives. His point was a wider (if not a larger or deeper) one. He was responding to the continued vitality of 'everyday religion' in the modern world. He goes on to say that, 'This sort of religion…was fated to be outgrown by the world's cultures, beginning with the West (specifically northern Europe) and then spreading across the globe, to be succeeded by a modern liberal faith sanctioned by (and providing sanction for) law, political theory, epistemology and science.'

Just to be clear, by 'modern liberal faith' he means that kind of faith or spirituality that is carefully separated away from public life, and especially from politics. According to the ideologues of modernism, religion was supposed to fade away to become, at best, what John Bowker (1987) called 'licensed insanities', i.e. utterly private (if profoundly personal) ideas in the hearts or souls of individuals that should not affect their voting or lobbying of politicians or their acquiescence to paying taxes. But religion has refused to fade away or to be shut away in cosy sanatoriums. Indeed, in the past 20 years or so we have seen many re-assertions of the presence of religion in public places including, but not only in, conflict zones. When broadcast media use terms like 'radical' or 'extremist' to describe some religiously motivated activity, they are playing along with the notion that religion should not direct ways in which people might wish to build communities, run their lives, resist the schizophrenic separation of private from public, and so on. For Orsi, it is not only such public religion that is an anomaly confronting what modernity proposed, but also 'everyday religion' in which people, seemingly everywhere, continue to display religious affiliations in jewellery, costume and car bumper-stickers, celebrate colourful and dramatic festivals, and consume meals together according to religious rules and etiquette.

Of particular importance in relation to this book, people continue to venerate the dead. Why is that particularly curious? If religion altogether was supposed to have been outgrown as modernity's putative rationalism spread, it might be obvious that odd ideas and ritualism about the dead should have disappeared. But honouring the dead is not a simple add-on or aside here. A solid part of the foundations of modernity was the Protestant Christian rejection of the medieval idea of the 'communion of saints' (i.e. that the living and the dead could pray for each other as they formed one community worshipping their God). This may have begun as a family conflict between Protestants and Catholics about whether solitary faith or shared activities are at the heart of true religion. Soon and easily, however, it became linked to the modernising insistence that we are all individuals. At any rate, one of the key acts of Reform across Europe was the official assault on ways of honouring the dead (saints or souls). Therefore, the book you are reading is about one aspect of a potentially challenging development at the heart of the contemporary world: the rediscovery of the importance of relationships between the living and the ancestors. Some will insist that it is entirely possible to honour the dead in secular ways; that this need not be about religion. I would agree entirely if I did not think that we have inherited an odd view of religion. The kind of richer understanding this book offers of the many things 'ancestors' might mean (both as ideas and in relation to activities and lifeways) may just contribute to an improved understanding of religion as a term for our relationships with a larger-than-modern and larger-than-human world.

Bibliography

Bowker, John 1987. *Licensed Insanities: Religions and Belief in God in the Contemporary World*. London, Darton, Longman and Todd.

Harvey, Graham 2013. *Food, Sex and Strangers: Understanding Religion as Everyday Life*. Routledge, London.

Orsi, Robert, A., 1997. 'Everyday Miracles: The Study of Lived Religion' in Hall, David, D. (ed.), *Lived Religion in America: Toward a History of Practice*. Princeton University Press, Princeton: 3-21.

Introduction

By Paul Davies

Our shared ancestors are with us now. They always have been. Present in mind, in the body of earth and in the spirit of their own selves, they stand with us loving, supporting and trying to guide our often clumsy attempts to negotiate the world in which we live. Their bodies are part of this earth and this earth is equally part of us – in flesh, in DNA as much as in spirit. In this way, we are the ancestors reborn. I like that thought, and that's how I arrived at this book.

Following a public campaign for the reburial of human remains at Avebury, the idea of a collective ancestry was introduced to the nation through a public consultation. Debates raged over identity and when the furore over Avebury eventually cooled down, a healthy interest in ancestry and all things ancestral blossomed. Pagans in Eire protested over the disturbance of ancestral remains at Tara, at Stonehenge in Wiltshire artists paraded a huge, 25ft tall effigy of the ancestor at sunrise. The lost ancestors of the lost circle at Charmy Down, Bath, were rediscovered and debates were held at museums in Manchester, Leicester and Oxford. The guardian ancestor of the underworld at Wookey Hole, Somerset, was honoured in ritual commemoration and the local and national media, with a brief interest, covered calls for reburial. As initiates embraced the ancestors and shone their spiritual light upon a newly expressed identity, people touched the earth and rediscovered a sense of self as part of the spirit of place.

This collection of wonderful essays extends these ideas about ancestry beyond reburial and goes some way to describing and addressing the eternal quest for spiritual identity in a fundamentally secular world. And quests, whether they be of the intellect or of a more physical journey, simply seek to express ideas and maybe our sense of belonging in shared landscapes. The authors themselves all describe in different ways the threefold relationship between self, ancestors and the landscapes in which we live and those we journey into. They are reflections of self. These, sometimes intimate, mirrors offer glimpses into colourful ways of thinking and being that can touch our hearts and help awaken within us forgotten or disregarded relationships with nature and our forebears. And that re-connection is what this book is all about really. A romantic idea? Certainly and unashamedly so, but one that is also academically and spiritually meaningful, and meaning is everything.

The first two chapters by Emma and Greywolf describe, very beautifully, their own connections to land and ancestor. Their primary roles in modern Paganism are that of ancestral advocates giving a voice to those who are not able to speak for themselves. Emma's melancholic piece delves bravely into an ancestral theology asking, 'What happens when we die?' and then insists upon a greater respect for our ancestors. Here, Emma's story is told and she seeks equality. Her work with Honouring the Ancient Dead and natural burial expresses the convictions of her belief. Camelia's eulogy (sometimes serious, sometimes funny) is vital and acknowledges that ancestry is all about our relationships with those who have gone before us as much as it is about those who return to find us, sometimes when we least expect it. Hers is memory and forgetting, of place and no place, of yew and you. Greywolf reveals a world that blurs any distinction between self and spirits. Are, I wonder, his Grey Wolf 'ghosts' singular or collective of a species? They are certainly his beautiful family and fiercely so.

Jenny and Robert then explore the Heathen tradition they both embraced, although I hazard a guess that this Heathenism chose them rather than anything else. Jenny's detailed paper describes some of the complexities of this northern tradition and she weaves her own personal ancestry in with that of the ancestral deities themselves. That kind of autobiography (or auto-ethnography) is a common thread throughout this book, where spirits or objects considered 'extra-ordinary', 'sacred' or 'deity' are now reconsidered in the light of ancestry. Distinctions blur, meanings shift and change and something inside seems to shine and say, 'Yes, that's it, exactly', or, 'Maybe...something else very close to that anyway.' For both Robert and Jenny, respect is a key factor, although how this is actually negotiated is sometimes a moot point. As anthropologists/archaeologists with more than a good grounding in material culture, these two authors are best placed to understand the imaginative and meaningful processes of identity as it more fully emerges through its expression – our very own genesis of culture. Critics outside the anthropology of modern Paganism, and there are many, often miss that point, confusing imaginative with invention.

Caitlín acknowledges the journey of pilgrimage as one important way of reconnecting to our ancestors. This connection is healing and, again, a theme prevalent that pops up here and there in the book. David Loxley, Chief of the usually silent Druid Order (AOD) explains different ways of understanding ancestors in the present tense in opposition to the usual 'ones who have gone before'. David's ancestor as triad is described in true pre-classical style, as he reaches toward ancient Egypt, and the unspoken letter here is T, Thoth or Taranis of the oak groves. Ronald's afterword offers a timely reminder that, as the ancients become ancient and therefore more venerable, our ancestors nevertheless made many mistakes and life choices resulting in consequences we are now having to deal with. We are facing a crisis, and here I refer to the general violence against nature and the *need* to move toward more environmentally and economically sustainable way of living. Acts of love and collective campaigning will get us there eventually. Penny's chapter shines with the light specific to the Order of Bards, Ovates and Druids and, like Caitlín and David, suggests meditation. All three offer different 'pathworkings' that seek unity and suggest a wholeness.

Luzie reminds us how we all share DNA (much more than was originally thought) and how the benefits of science really are complementary to spiritual enquiry. Spain, Italy and the Balkan peninsula are the ancestral landscapes of the English oak, while wheat originated further away in the Fertile Crescent. Luzie names Turkey, but the area also covers Iraq, Iran, Syria and Palestine. Her genetic world is inclusive of bluebells, jays and retreating ice sheets. Hold that thought. Finally, and without apology, I include here a chapter about Quaker values and worship within nature (that's worship within, not worship of, nature). Sarah reminds us that ancestry is not the sole concern of Druids, Heathens, healers, archaeologists nor social anthropologists. Her experience of urbanity and the ancestral landscapes of Suffolk and Kent are of colourful soundscapes filled with living history. And so, ancestry is indeed shared and understood by many spiritualities, in many ways. That seems so important. To have variety and difference of opinion without conflict or abuse is the way forward, and always has been. With most Quakers having their spiritual history rooted within love and peace and light (with a great emphasis on peace), I am reminded of how Christianity is itself legitimised in part by an ancestral tradition of saints and other historical figures, many of whom perform, or were said to have once performed, miraculous feats. They may be considered lesser spiritual deities beneath the wing of the heavenly triad, the one God. A very Pagan path to follow.

Graham has the first word and speaks of an emerging and startling veneration and Ronald has the last, suggesting we all seek ways to apply our knowledge for a greater benefit and without prejudice. I am not at all averse to expressing these ideas in ways that are both secular and sacred.

The sun is shining upon the earth, and the frosts are, once more, retreating. The wind is rising and the mists will come. Time to touch the earth again. It seems so long since I have done that. Wheat grain is sprouting from the soil and I pray the acorns will produce saplings this year, although I fear they may not. The birds are interested in what I'm doing (humans don't usually touch the earth and sit in silence listening). Perhaps they are waiting for more seed. I recall a recent National Geographic article I stumbled upon while Googling, which described how dinosaurs were once covered in feathers. They evolved, perhaps, into dunnocks and blackbirds and herons and jackdaws. That makes me wonder about the processes of evolution, the 'past in present' and how, in the *here and now* when the idea of ancestry is fully embodied within ourselves and in our own spiritual practices, those distinctions/separations really do seem to lose their meaning (or perhaps it is truer to say that they are transformed).

Touch the earth and think of the womb from which we are reborn and, silently, she may answer. Ancestry is like that and has contained within it ideas that have many meanings and much potential. That is a spirituality best understood as 3D poetry, better expressed in surreal form, and that art is *ritual*.

In Peace,

Oddie

Time and the Grave

By Emma Restall Orr

The fellow lifts himself heavily from the bench, and turns to me with a smile bruised and battered with grief. We hold hands for a while, our breath misty in the cold air, no more words needed. As he trudges away I watch, his feet scuffing the stones of the track. He stops by his car and I wait, alert with concern, but slowly he lifts a hand, and with an extraordinary tenderness he touches the hazel catkins that hang, honey-yellow, in the frosty grey of the leafless hedge. I see him breathe in, nod to himself, before getting into the car and quietly driving away.

What happens to us when we die?

It's a question that lingers. At the natural burial ground where I work it is a question that is posed every day. Those who are facing their own demise, who are searching for what it will take to let go in peace, with grace, will often stare into the darkness of the not-knowing. Those who are floundering after the physical loss of a loved one, who feel the emptiness in their arms, yet the bursting fullness in their hearts, will cry out to me, knowing it is a question that can't really be answered. Those finding a way of living when their worlds have been reshaped by death, stand at the graveside and stare.

Detailed assertions have for aeons been put forward by the religious, the spiritual, the philosophical, the scientific, offering answers, both comforting and dreadful. That these are so diverse only fuels the agnostics' dilemma, provoking many simply to shrug, resigned to the enormity of their ignorance, while others stride towards denial, refusing to think of the inevitable, that death comes to us all. Yet the question persists. Our mortality, and how we carry it, plays a significant role in what makes us

11

who we are.

When someone tells me they have no fear of death, I hear words that clatter with what seems to me a graceless irreverence. Death is not a force about which we should risk any expression of hubris. We may feel comfortable with the idea of our own personal journey, confident that we will be peaceful in our courage should we know when death approaches. We may even feel assured that our affairs are sufficiently in order so that, were we to die today, we would leave little that would burden others, tidying up the debris of our lives. But for most of us, this is not the case. Death frequently brings with it terrible pain and disorder. Not only do many die having crawled through long hours of suffering, but seldom do we die before someone dies whom we love dearly. Death then reaches deep inside us, merciless, hollowing out a vast, empty cavity of grief. How we spend our finite years, with death behind us, death beside us, death before us, how we carry the certainty of death, helps to shape us.

As thinking beings, aware of ourselves as thinking beings, it is the mind that many are primarily concerned with: when we die, does the 'I' head off upon its next adventure, or is it extinguished? These two alternative beliefs are the most common within our culture, the first a substance dualism, where the soul or spirit leaves the physical body, the second a materialist monism, where there is nothing but matter, the mind being no more than a chemical phenomenon.

Then there's the other side of the question, which is not so ethereal. When we die, what will happen to the fleshy parcel that is our physical body? What we would want for ourselves, and for those we care for, is informed by our understanding of the I. If the body, after death, has no spirit, no soul, no mind, then it is effectively just detritus, the organic remains or leavings after a life of conscious living. We shouldn't care what happens to it. For without a subject, a perceiving I, it is an object, a thing, no more than inert matter.

Of course, although some quip that their family should not bother with the fuss of a funeral, that their body should be thrown out with the rubbish sacks, there are forces that don't allow this. Religious strictures, and legal requirements, ensure that what happens to the dead is socially responsible. But there is more: in a healthy human being there is an emotional desire to ensure that the body of one who has died is properly cared for. Even the committed dualist who believes the soul to have flown, even the ardent materialist who believes the person no longer exists, can feel some degree of continuing concern, an impulse to care.

At what point does that fall away?

Let me now change the tone and direction of this brief essay, and offer here two words, words that, like many with equally ancient Germanic roots, have a deftly effective impact: wet and dry. There is a significant difference between the newly deceased, still fleshed, soft, cold and heavy, perhaps seeping with potentially dangerous fluids, with whom we still have some relationship, the wet dead; and the dry dead, the stale old bones of the long dead, discarnate, faceless, and now relatively safe.

Consider this within our modern culture. In our heavily populated country, we are encouraged to hand over those who are dying into the care of hospitals, nursing homes and hospices, to hand over the dead to funeral directors, keeping death at arms' length: death is no longer a natural and inexorable part of everyday life in every home. Most now have no idea how to deal with the wet dead, physically or emotionally, the driving instinct being to step away. In Britain more than 70 per cent have their loved ones cremated, the long process of natural release and transformation now exchanged for 90 minutes at 1,000°C. A few days later the ashes are returned to the funeral director. No longer a person, the wet is now dry. Instead of daily or weekly visits to the cemetery, the urn stays with the funeral director, or in the back of a cupboard, or perhaps one day the ashes are scattered somewhere that feels right, usually at a significant distance from home. Grief is a bore: we feel the pressure not to tire others with the burden of our loss, but to accept and move on: he's dead, dry, gone.

How our culture deals with the ancient dead is a reflection of this. Bones disinterred through the process of land development are bagged up as 'human remains': the dry dead. Faceless, nameless, they may be packed into boxes, and taken to some archaeological store, perhaps accessioned into a museum's collection. The intention may be to study or rebury, according to the requirements of the exhumation licence, but many will disappear with the hundreds of thousands of other ancestral bones, down some crevice created by an ever-increasing lack of resources, abandoned on shelves for decades to come.

At the same time, archaeologists dig up graves as entertainment for popular television shows, making wild speculations, telling stories, as if the act of ransacking a grave were entirely acceptable, good clean fun: it is the dry dead they are finding, not the wet. Furthermore, despite new 3D replication technology, museums still believe it acceptable to create displays using the bones of individual people, mocking up the opened grave, manipulating a skeleton into a pose, provoking visitors with a little shock and horror in brightly-lit cases. Or, where they have only disarticulated bones, a femur is placed as another object in a museum gallery. A cranium lies on a glass shelf in a display cabinet, alongside shards of pottery, an old knife, a small card with a few abstruse words, all historical artefacts, dull and dry. The person is not a person: the bone is just another item of interest.

What happens to us when we die?

The question is then extended to this: when we choose to bury a loved one, when we lay someone to rest, with the prayers and grace of whatever ritual we need, in the presence of our family, our friends, our God(s), do we expect that person to be left to rest in peace? If so, for how long? The Human Tissues Act (2004) was written into UK legislation in response to a scandal about children's organs that had been retained and studied without consent: wet flesh. Its remit covers one hundred years. Those who have died more than a century ago were felt to have slipped out of memory, no longer to be in relationship with the living. Even organs preserved in jars, if old enough, were somehow now considered to be of the dry dead.

Yet, a hundred years after the start of the Great War, its anniversaries are bringing back to us not just pertinent imagery, but stories, memories, the names of grandfathers, great uncles, great grandfathers, great grandmothers, together with photographs that reveal faces. Poppies floating in the Thames wet the edges of the dry dead, changing their status, calling these individuals back into our hearts, giving them space within the communities and families of the living. We can again hear their laughter, acknowledge their love and pain. They have become persons again. Jack Cooper, a young lad of 18, a farm labourer until he stepped up to volunteer, who as a soldier died slowly, terribly, in the dreadful stench of no-man's land somewhere in northern France, his right leg blown off just above the knee: were his bones to be found by the plough, and exhumed by archaeologists, would it be acceptable to put them on display? Whose consent would it be necessary to achieve, or could it be done without consent?

Let's consider another lad, this one 14 years old, his muscles strong from working on the land, his form short and slight from being always hungry. His bones are found when a field-edge ditch is dug more deeply after flooding. After initial concern about murder, the bones indicating multiple stab wounds, the police pathologists acknowledge their age, and pass them over to archaeologists. Everything points to a battle of the Civil War, from which perhaps the young lad crawled away, hiding himself in a gulley where he later died, to be lost for 370 years. We don't know his name, but still we can picture his life, amidst a landscape before the enclosures, pulling oxen along the ridge and furrow of the great Warwickshire Feldon, laughing with his brothers, looking forward to lifting the flagon of sun-warmed, sharp, home-brewed cider that will quench his thirst. Would it be acceptable to put his dry, cracked bones on display in a museum? If, instead of being left in the ditch, when the fighting was over one of the local women picking over the battlefield had found him, if he'd been returned to his home and buried, his mother weeping at the grave, would it be acceptable to exhume him, for the sake of scientific curiosity or a television show?

What change would be required for it to be defensible to do so?

Perhaps there is something poignant about having an entire skeleton. If all that had been found by that French plough were a femur or a cranium, the dead soldier remaining without identification, or if the English boy who had died in that Warwickshire ditch had been scattered by time and wildlife, leaving just a few bones, would that make a difference?

What if we were able to identify the person whose cranium sits on the shelf on display in the museum? A woman in her mid 20s, with three living children, three having died, we can imagine her, a lass with long fair hair, sitting in the meadow by the river, the baby at her breast, breaking hunks of bread and cheese for the older two boys, laughing as they chase butterflies in the sunshine. Her name is Hancara: she was wife of the tanner Catacus, whose beautiful voice following her death would sing nothing but laments. Putting flesh on her dry bones, she becomes an individual once more, a warm and tender human being, loving mother, daughter, wife. Can you feel the softness of her cheek as she embraces you, still laughing? Of course, such a story can be discarded as pure fiction. Yet, only the little details are gathered from thin air: the individual whose cranium is on that museum shelf was no less a real, living, breathing, laughing human being.

Is it time that makes the difference? The Human Tissues Act speaks of 'deceased persons', while museums and archaeologists working with older ancestors refer merely to 'human remains'. King Richard III, whose bones were exhumed from a car park in 2012, died in 1485; however, his social status sets him apart, allowing him to be laid to rest in Leicester Cathedral, with dignity and grace, and in a manner that ensures he will not be disturbed again. Is it the lack of a name then, or the absence of memories, that diminishes a person's individuality, a person's humanity, sufficiently to make it acceptable to pull them from the grave, to keep in boxes or exhibit their bones as curiosities?

For some, such as myself, it is never acceptable. For some, the exhibiting of ancestors is in every case deemed indecorous, the retention of the dead in museum and archaeological storerooms is felt to be wholly disrespectful. To dig up a grave is always an unjustifiable act of desecration. There never comes a point where the dead lose their personhood. It makes no difference at all whether they died five years ago or five thousand years. But why?

Returning to that original question is a place to start: what happens to us when we die? I spoke of the two most common beliefs, the dualist and materialist, both of which consider the physical body as inert matter at death. To an animist such as myself, there is quite a different standpoint, based on an integrationist metaphysical perspective of a universe that is undivided. What is generally perceived as the distinction between mind and matter is understood by the animist as an illusion created by the veil of perception. In other words, the limitations of the human mind mean that we can never perceive nature as it actually is, but only as we perceive it to be through the rough filters of our senses, the way in which we process that data having evolved purely to support the simple needs of survival. Our basic awareness is of mind being something separate from matter, but nature, as it is in itself, is whole: the experience of the individual mind emerges because the essence of nature is minded.

Animism is considered by the ill-informed to be no more than a primitive and superstitious nonsense, a childlike view of trees that talk. It is nothing of the kind. With a strong heritage worldwide, including in Western philosophy, it has an entirely rational foundation, overcoming the unavoidable problems found in both materialist and dualist metaphysics. Where the basis of the universe is an essential consciousness, all that comes into form within nature is conscious, from the layers that exist within what we term subatomic particles, out to galaxies and the dark matter that many believe may constitute the greater part of the universe. Wherever that mindedness coheres, becoming moments of being, there are patterns of perpetual interaction, of perceiving and responding. Human consciousness is just one specific and unimaginably narrow version of the countless perspectives within the wholeness of nature. It is the only type of consciousness we have, the only one we know, and indeed perhaps the only one that we can even begin to imagine.

This animism does not explain beyond doubt the mystery of death. In some ways it adds to the enigma, for in recognising the limits of human consciousness, it emphasises all that we cannot know. However, what it offers is an idea of how we are as we are, through the journey of living. For during our lives, from our first years, we slowly build and determine our sense of self, the I that perceives, the I that allows us the experience of our own existence. Yet the coherence of being that makes up the self isn't contained solely within a physical body: it extends, reaching out through communication, building with each action and reaction, each relationship, each act of creativity and participation, as connections and memories develop and spread. We grow, becoming more fully a part of the woven fabric of the worlds in which we live, until the centre of that self begins to soften in focus. Slowly, with age or disease that softening accelerates, leaving the I less and less substantial, this dissolving continuing through our journey of dying, and on through the days and years after we have died. Slowly, softly, the I lets go, releasing itself from the coherence of individuality, and returning to the wholeness of nature in itself.

The purpose of this essay, however, is not to present an exposition of animist metaphysics, nor to justify it as a philo-sophical position, but to explain why such a perspective may lead to such strong attitudes about the dead. This sense of nature's wholeness is key. From an animist perspective, the world is not empty space and inert matter, through which a select number of sentient beings move. There are no things, there are no objects. Every part of the universe, from the subatomic to the cosmic, is in a state of perpetual experience, wakefully engaging in relationship within each ecosystem, with each momentary interaction a note in the song of the whole. It is this ongoing sensation of mindful wholeness that so comprehen-sively informs the fundamental beliefs.

In this respect, the dead are not absent. Again, it isn't necessary to resort to the childish picture of a ghost, nor the dualist's wandering spirit, but to consider instead the animist's awareness of nature. Within the wholeness of nature, each ecosystem is vibrant with countless wakeful interactions, each one flowing into effects and memories. As such, a person does not leave their tribe when they die, they do not lose their place within their community of family and friends. Their stories still hum in the air. Relationships continue to evolve, their presence still affecting and influencing the living.

The dead fall from awareness only when they are forgotten, so the practising animist acknowledges the ancestors with gratitude and open-heartedness, each and every day – whenever a task is to be done, whenever an old tool is lifted, a skill used, an old pathway walked. When a challenge or an obstacle arises blocking the way, when pain kicks in and weakness overwhelms, it is to the ancestors that the animist turns, and it is in the ancestors that courage is found, generation to generation, hand in hand, words of wisdom heard and experience shared. When crises are overcome, when love is found and joy fills a moment with delight, the ancestors are an integral part of the celebration.

The wholeness of nature means that it is not purely the ancestors of a person's blood that are held with grace. In any landscape, the hedgerows and trees, the field boundaries, the buildings, tracks and roads, all tell of ancestral lives. The landscapes of the human mind are equally important, shaped by discovery and belief, knowledge and assumption. As an animist, my sense is that to forget the ancestors' presence is a foolish mistake, but worse is to forget to acknowledge them with respect: for in doing so, we take for granted what we have, and what we have can then be easily and quickly lost.

The wholeness of nature is also reflected in an integrated understanding of time. We cannot know what time is within nature beyond the veil of our human perception, but we can speculate that the flow as we experience it is simply a tool honed by evolution to facilitate our survival. Many different schools of thought suggest time is not as linear as it appears to be. To the animist, meditating on nature's completeness, time transforms into presence. The ancestors are not dislocated from us, in some past that is dead and gone: their presence can be felt, and their influence continues.

If we return then to Hancara and Jack Cooper, and – let's name the lad who died in 1642, say – Bart Hancox, the centuries between them become incidental. That Hancara died a thousand years before Bart does not make her any less a person loved and lost. She is no more 'human remains' than those individuals we ourselves have known, whom we have loved, who have died in our own lifetimes, whom we grieve. They are persons, as is every individual whose bones and cremated ash are packed away in boxes in museums, archaeological units, hospital laboratories, historical societies and anywhere else, or placed on a museum shelf as an exhibit to be peered at or ignored.

I kneel on the damp grass beside a grave, the mound of earth starting to settle a week having now past since the funeral took place. The three large bouquets are looking tatty, the winter weather having taken its toll, and gently I pull them apart, separating the strands of pussy willow, rosemary and spruce from the frosted lilies and roses, finding the odd piece of sea holly, creating a single new arrangement and making a heap for the compost. As I work, I sing, my breath misty in the cold air, and I chatter and I sing, not just to the fellow buried before me, but to others also laid to rest in this place. My focus is drawn to the soft call of a fieldfare in the hedgerow, talking to his kin. A dunnock hops between the tussocks and saplings nearby, occasionally pausing to listen.

What happens to us when we die?

Tying the bouquet with raffia, I lay it on the grave with an affirmation of peace, and as I gather up the frosted flower stems, I ponder on how radiant the petals were just a few days before. Within the timeless whole that is nature, it is so often in impermanence, in the ever-changing tides of emergence and evanescence, of living and dying, of blossom and decay, that we find the most intense beauty. In grief, we find wonder in the first catkins of spring. At the compost heap, I up-end the trug.

Decay is as integral a part of nature as growth, winter as crucial as summer to the balance within this landscape. Trying to preserve something from decay is to create a pool of stagnation. In the same way, there is no need for a belief in the immortality of the soul, nor affirmations of individuality that raise someone above the crowd: for a while we exist in form, a form our human consciousness perceived as mind and body, but it is just for a while before we dissolve back into the eternal whole. Or so I believe.

What happens to this thinking I, this centre of me, will actually remain a mystery to me until, perhaps, the day I die. Whatever happens, I will be thankful for the presence of the ancestors, asserting the importance of that gratitude and the need for true respect.

Tribes of Spirit: Animals as Ancestors

By Greywolf

And those two dogs of thine, Yama, the watchers, four-eyed, who look on men and guard the pathway, Entrust this man, O King, to their protection, and with prosperity and health endow him. Dark-hued, insatiate, with distended nostrils, Yama's two envoys roam among the People; May they restore to us a fair existence here and to-day, that we may see the sunlight.
(Author unknown, c.1500-1200 BCE)

Long ago, K'wati, the Transformer, came to a place where a forest of huge cedar trees grew alongside a river that flowed into a great ocean. Finding no humans there, but many wolves, K'wati changed some of the wolves into humans and told them they would always be strong and brave because they were descended from wolves.

This is the origin story of the Native American Quileute tribe, whose name means 'Wolf People'. They still inhabit part of their ancestral lands on the north-west Pacific coast of the Olympic Peninsula in Washington State, where archaeology shows their forebears to have lived for at least 8,000 years. Before settlers of European descent (the Quileute called them *ho-kwats*, drifting house people) arrived to annexe their land, fell their forests, wipe out their game animals, over-fish their waters, outlaw their language and ban their spiritual practices, Quileute society centred around four societies, each with its own ceremonies, songs and dances. These were the Wolf warrior society, the Fishing society, the Whale-Hunters' society and the Game-Hunters society.

The Wolf warrior society ceremonies were called *T'lok'wali*. At the beginning of the Wolf Ceremony, members behaved as wolves, howling and prowling in the temperate rain forest that covers much of their former lands. Members of the society then entered a ceremonial longhouse, still in their Wolf *personae*. During the five-day ceremony they sang songs, some handed down through families, others given by guardian spirits. This reflects the two types of membership of the tribal societies, one paid for by family members and the other for those who received visitations from one of the guardian spirits of the society they were to join (Frachtenberg 1921).

This is relevant to me for several reasons. I have my own connection with a guardian Wolf spirit who came to me in southern England in 1994 during a sweat lodge on a Druid camp. The lodge was a low dome constructed from bent hazel poles and covered with tarpaulins. This style of construction is used by native peoples of the North American plains, notably the Lakota, but was also used by our ancestors in Bronze Age Britain (Hutton 2013). Our sweat lodge on the Druid camp was led by Georgien Wybenga, a Dutch woman taught by a Lakota medicine man, Archie Fire Lame Deer.

In the crowded darkness and overwhelming heat of the lodge, Georgien introduced us to animal guardians of the four quarters. One was Coyote. Knowing that coyote had never been native to the British Isles, I wondered what our native equivalent would be. Given the trickster nature of Coyote in Native American legends, the obvious British equivalent would be Fox. However, the animal who appeared to me was a Wolf. Big, muscular and stockily built, he lay curled in the pit in the centre of the lodge. The hot rocks onto which water was poured to create steam were glowing inside his body. He stood, still with the dully glowing rocks inside him and, with a flick of his head, gestured for me to follow him.

Leaving my body, I followed the Wolf outside. There, instead of the flat English summer field in which we had built our lodge, I found myself on the lower slopes of a snow-covered mountain.

Some way off was the edge of a forest. The Wolf again gestured for me to follow, turned and paced off through the snow, his paws leaving clear prints. I tried to place my human feet in his paw-prints. At the time, my conscious thought was that I did this in order to preserve the pristine whiteness of the snow. In retrospect, I see that it was part of the process of aligning myself with the spirit of the Wolf.

At a steady, loping pace the Wolf soon covered the distance between the lodge and the tree line, me following. I was naked, as my body had been in the sweat lodge, yet I felt no cold. At the tree line, huge conifers towered above us, growing so thickly that it was impossible to see too far into the forest before the darkness became impenetrable. The Wolf paused at the beginning of a well-worn track that wound away beneath the trees and vanished into shadow. He led me a short way along the track then turned to face me. Speaking directly into my mind, he told me I should go back to my body, but that next time we met he would lead me further into the forest. He told me his name before walking away.

I returned the way we had come, following the tracks in the snow. They still looked like paw-prints, with little sign of my human footfalls. Rejoining my body in the lodge, the heat, previously almost unbearable, now seemed tempered from the memory of the cold outside.

Next morning the fire-keeper for the lodge, Walter, suggested I should try to find some memento of a wolf to provide a tangible link to my vision. I thought this unlikely. I'd lived for 40 years never once seeing hide nor hair, tooth nor claw of a wolf. Spirit, however, knew better.

Eight days after the lodge, I went to a garage sale held by a friend. On arrival, the first thing I saw was a huge pelt laying across an old water tank. I thought, 'That's wolf,' then, 'No, it can't be.' I asked my friend, Andy. 'I think it's wolf,' he said. It was indeed the hides of six wolves, sewn together as a rug. It had been in the house when Andy's parents bought it in 1947. They hadn't liked it, so stuffed it into a bag and stowed it in the loft. There it remained until Andy found it on the day of the sweat lodge. I told Andy's mother about my vision, and she gave me the rug. It was in good condition despite being around 50 years old. I removed its felt backing, added ties to it and began wearing it in ceremonies as a cloak.

Being a vegetarian at the time, I was taken aback when, a few days after receiving the cloak, I was invited to a venison feast. 'Well,' I thought, 'I may be vegetarian but these wolves who have come to me aren't, so I shall eat for them.' Our host knew the hunter who had killed the stag whose meat we were to eat. He told us the story of the hunt in fine bardic style. The venison had been hung for a few days then steeped overnight in red wine. I was wearing the wolf-skin cloak and, as the first mouthful of tender, succulent meat slid down my throat, I felt a powerful ripple run through the hides and they began to give off heat. It was an extraordinary feeling, as these long-dead wolves were reborn on my body.

The Wolf who had come to me in the sweat lodge became both a working partner and an *alter ego*. A regular part of my spiritual practice was to switch bodies with him. The first time it happened I was surprised to say the least. A few weeks after he first came to me, I needed to journey into the spirit world to help a friend. I called upon 'my' Wolf. He appeared a few yards away, fixed his gaze on mine and bounded at me with such speed that I had no time to react. His body smacked into mine and passed through it. As it did so, my consciousness switched into him, leaving his consciousness in my body. Suddenly I was a Wolf, with greatly enhanced senses and my visual perspective lowered from being on all fours.

My sense of what was, or was not, important shifted radically too. My whole being focused only on what needed to be done, nothing more. All the extraneous concerns one has while being human were gone. Being solely concentrated on the task at hand meant that it was performed with speed and efficiency far greater than the human 'I' was capable of. It was a salutary lesson. As humans, we compile such complex tangles of thoughts and feelings around each and every aspect of our lives that we are often frozen into inaction. Wolves have no such problem. They do what they need to do, when they need to do it, with complete focus and clarity.

Through the wolf-skin cloak, my alter-ego and I found ourselves with an adopted pack of six young Wolves. This proved invaluable when encountering Otherworldly beings whose strengths were greater than ours. The pack were there in an instant when called, a powerful whirlwind of fur, teeth and claws, snapping and snarling when needed, though most creatures encountered were so intimidated by their appearance that they turned tail and fled, making further confrontation unnecessary.

The pack protect and care for each other. Wolves are social animals. For much of the year, they hunt in packs. They share child-rearing, looking after each others' cubs. Kills are shared according to a pack hierarchy dominated by the alpha male and female. When I became Wolf, I was the pack's alpha male. When I am human, my Wolf brother from the sweat lodge continues to fulfil that role.

Many wolf-related gifts came in the weeks and months following my initial vision; pictures of wolves, wolf stories and books, even a tooth. A chant was given to me during a Gorsedd ceremony among the ancient stone circles of Avebury, in Wiltshire. An American Druid, Ellen Evert Hopman, asked the hundred or so people taking part if we'd like to learn a Wolf song. Naturally, I was enthusiastic, and so were many others. Ellen taught us the chant, which she said came from the Seneca people of North America. I was delighted to have a song to sing that would provide another connection with my spirit Wolves.

Later, at another Druid camp, I sang the Wolf chant. Three people who'd been at Avebury the day Ellen gave it to us all agreed I'd got it wrong. They sat me down and taught it to me again. This time I was sure I'd got it. At the next event where I sung it, people again told me I'd got it wrong. Again, I tried to learn it. Again, I failed. After three attempts, I realised what was happening. My spirit had taken a Native American chant and converted it into something more local and personal, a Native British Wolf chant. I still use it today.[1]

This Native British Wolf chant brings us back to the Quileute, the Wolf People. In 2004, friends in Seattle arranged a trip out to the Olympic Peninsula for myself and my sons, Joe and Mike. We were to stay one night at La Push, the coastal village at the heart of the Quileute reservation. None of us knew anything about the tribe at the time. On arrival at La Push, we checked in to pick up the keys to our cabin. The woman at the desk said we were just in time for a potlatch feast at the village hall and that we should go. After a long drive, we were happy with the prospect, but had no idea what to expect. Arriving late, we found the feast already well under way. Trestle tables were set out in rows and it seemed the whole village was there. We were shown to a table and generous plates of cooked salmon were brought to us.

After the feast, another surprise: there was to be a drum circle. It so happened that I'd bought a new drum in Seattle a couple of days earlier and had it with me. Once the tables were cleared and chairs pushed back against the walls, the drum circle began. Vince Penn, leading the circle that night, explained that it was their tradition to ask the person from furthest away to speak first. He walked over to where I was lurking quietly in a corner and said, 'That's you.'

I was lost for words. Then I thought, 'Well, I've got my new drum, maybe I should do my Wolf chant?' Stepping out into the hall I said, 'My name's Greywolf, also known as Philip, and I have a Wolf chant I'd like to share with you.' I began to drum and then sing. The chant gradually gets faster and faster until it's impossible to keep up, at which point you howl. That's what I did. I had no idea how it would go down, but needn't have worried. The room fell silent for a second when I finished, then people spontaneously burst into applause.

The potlatch ceremony is a tradition of the Quileute and other tribes of the region in which members of the tribe recognise good things others have done for them by giving gifts. In this gift-giving, I noted that myself and my sons seemed to be getting more than our fair share. For me, the most precious gift came when Vince stepped into the centre carrying a T-shirt bearing a design one of the drum circle members had received in a vision. Vince held up the shirt and said that the members of the circle had decided to make me a member. He presented me with the shirt.

After the potlatch came the drumming. A group of nine or ten drummers gathered in a corner of the hall. As a new member of the circle, I joined them and, for the rest of the evening, did my best to keep time and join in with the songs as and when I could pick them up. Joe and Mike joined the village children in several of the dances. It was a joyous evening.

At the end of the circle, Vince's wife, Sharon, asked if we would come to her office the next morning. She told us where to find it, but we took a wrong turn and ended up driving through the village. Everyone we saw burst into smiles and waved heartily. We naturally smiled and waved back. Eventually we found Sharon's office, still having no idea what we were doing there. I thought maybe we'd committed some awful *faux pas* and were going to be told off for it. Memories of school days and the headmaster's office. In fact, Sharon gave drum circle T-shirts to my sons and said that they should also consider themselves members of the circle. She then told me a story.

The weekly meeting of tribal elders had taken place five days before we arrived. A few had already got there when one of the older members walked in and asked, 'Where's Greywolf?' The others had no idea what he meant, since there is no Greywolf amongst the elders. 'Do you mean Grey Eagle? He ain't here yet,' they said. 'No,' he responded, 'it's Greywolf, and he's either here or he's comin'.' Although I hadn't noticed at the time, when I stood in the circle and said my name was Greywolf, the elders sitting around the edge of the hall had pricked up their ears and looked from one to the other.

I felt I'd made a strong spiritual connection with the Quileute during that short visit. Ever since, I've regarded them as brothers and sisters, fellow members of the spirit Tribe of the Wolf.

As a child, the animal I identified with most was not wolf, but heron. I saw these silent grey, white and black birds standing alone at the side of the drainage ditches that criss-cross Romney Marsh, on the edge of which I lived. As an outsider, feeling little connection with either my own family or others of my own age, the solitary nature of the heron had a strong appeal. A heron is a long way from a wolf. However, there is the familiar concept of the lone wolf who prowls beyond the boundaries of the pack, seeking his own paths through the wilderness. This too could hardly fail to appeal. Where, though, does this stronger, deeper adult connection come from?

Though not widely known or acknowledged, we Europeans have ancestral traditions not unlike those of Native Americans and other indigenous peoples, many of which connect with animal spirits. The idea of animal possession as a way to gain extra-human abilities seems to be more-or-less universal, spanning the Old World and the New. Wolf or dog societies (the two often appear to be interchangeable in ritual contexts) seem to have existed among our Indo-European ancestors for at least 4,000 years, probably much longer. Evidence for one such group is set out in an article entitled 'Midwinter dog sacrifices and warrior initiations in the Late Bronze Age at the site of Krasnosamarskoe, Russia', detailing excavations carried out to the north of the Black Sea (Brown 2012). On this single site the remains of 51 dogs, seven wolves and six unidentified canines were found, outnumbering those of any other animal. The percentage of canine bones is about a hundred times that found at any other site in the region. The animals had been butchered during the winter months, though the site was inhabited year-round. Their skulls were dismembered in a distinctive, ritualised way unlike any other creatures in the same culture.

The archaeologists looked at linguistic and literary evidence for canine cults. This led them to conclude that, 'Wolves and dogs were the principal symbols of youthful war-bands composed of boys who had been initiated into a liminal intro-ductory period of warrior status,' citing as examples the Vedic *Vrātyas*, Roman *Luperci* (Wolf-brothers) and Irish *Fianna*. *Vrātyas* held a 12-day sacrificial ritual at midwinter (Brown 2012). *Luperci* were the leading celebrants in the wild rites of *Lupercalia* in ancient Italy, held in February. The authors believe similar sacri-ficial rites to have been held during the winter months across the whole range of Indo-European settlement. Given that the Quileute Wolf ceremony, and similar rites among other tribes, also took place in winter, I would argue that the range was considerably wider, suggesting an origin that pre-dates the development of Indo-European culture circa 7,000 years ago. This view is supported by Karl Schlesier, who details numerous similarities between Cheyenne Wolf ceremonies and similar ones among Siberian peoples, positing a common origin for both going back at least 12,000 years (Schlesier 2013).

Bearing in mind the Bronze Age Russian ceremonial site referred to above, it's interesting to note that Schlesier's account of the five-day Cheyenne Massaum ceremony includes the ritual consumption of cooked dog-meat (Schlesier 2013: 99). In both cases, the consumption of dog meat goes completely against accepted social norms, which is precisely its point. The act is doubly transgressive for a Wolf person in that, for us, eating dog is a form of cannibalism. Transgressing a deeply held taboo helps place such rituals in a category far removed from everyday life, a liminal area of experience where anything becomes possible, where boundaries between worlds break down and passage between them can be achieved with comparative ease.

Reinforcing the liminal associations of the canine species we find numerous spiritual world-views in which dogs guard entrances to the realms of the dead or accompany deities who guide the recently dead to their Otherworld homes. We have already encountered the Hindu God Yama and his two dogs 'who look on men and guard the pathway'. The ancient Greeks knew the land of the dead ruled over by Hades to be guarded by the three-headed dog Cerberus. The ancient Egyptian God of death and guide of the souls of the dead is jackal-headed Anubis, while the Meso-American Toltec people honoured a similar dog-headed deity named Xolotl.

An early instance of an individual in Britain connecting with Wolf spirits lies in a glass case in the Wiltshire Archaeology and Natural History Society Museum in Devizes, near where I live. This is a necklace, anklet or bracelet, made using 17 pierced canine teeth from adult wolves, and one from a dog. It was recovered from a Bronze Age burial in a bowl barrow excavated by William Cunnington in 1805 and identified as South Newton G1. The same grave contained an amber bead and traces of what may have been a bronze dagger. Given the difficulty of gathering so many teeth from a single wild species, we may assume that this individual felt a very strong link with wolves. From its context, this burial probably dates to somewhere between 2400 and 1500 BCE.

Traces of Wolf clans, societies and individuals survive in British and Irish records. Cunobelinos, who ruled much of south-east England in the 1st century, has a name meaning 'Wolf of [the God] Belinos'. He is the origin of Shakespeare's Cymbeline. Other names from the Romano-British era include Cunovendus, 'Bright

Wolf', and Cunobarrus, 'Wolf Chief'. The 'cu' or 'cuno' element found in many Celtic names is often translated as 'hound', but seems originally to have meant 'wolf'.

Irish wolf names include Faolán (Wolf), Anglicised as Fillin or Phelan, as well as the legendary hero Cúchulainn and various Conors, Conns, Conans and others. Bearing in mind what we've seen about the consumption of dog meat only in special ritual circumstances in Bronze Age Russia and 19th century America, it's worth noting that Cúchulainn's death resulted partly from his breaking a taboo (Irish *geis*) placed on him that prohibited him from eating the flesh of canines (O'hOgain 1990). The Welsh Bleddyn, Anglicised as Blethin, also means 'Wolf'. Britain's ancient collection of legends, the *Mabinogi*, contains several instances of shape-shifting. In the story of *Math, son of Mathonwy*, the eponymous enchanter turns the God Gwydion and his brother, Gilvaethwy, into mated pairs of animals, including wolves. As a wolf, Gilvaethwy gives birth to a pup who becomes a human child when Math restores the brothers to their human forms. The child is named Bleiddwn, 'Wolf' (Davies 2007). Perhaps modern-day Bleddyns and Blethins are also descended from this mythical shape-shifter.

The hero of the early English poem Beowulf has a name meaning 'Bee-Wolf', a poetic reference to the honey-loving bear.[2] Norse examples of wolf-names include Thorolf, 'Wolf of Thor', and Randwulf (later Randolph), 'Shield Wolf'. There were Wolf warriors among the pre-Christian Scandinavians, members of animal-centred cults linked with Odin, a shape-shifting shaman God often accompanied by two wolves, Geri and Freki (Ravenous and Greedy). Snorri Sturluson, in *Ynglinga Saga*, describes these warriors as follows:

[Odin's] men went to battle without armour and acted like mad dogs or wolves. They bit into their shields and were as strong as bears or bulls. They killed men, but neither fire nor iron harmed them. This madness is called berserker-fury. (Byock 1998)

Wolf-warriors called *Úlfhéðnar* (singular *Úlfheðinn*) are mentioned in the *Vatnsdœla saga*, *Haraldskvæði* and *Völsunga saga*. *Úlfheðinn* means 'Wolf-tunic', much as the better-known *Berserker* means 'Bear-shirt'. Both seem to refer to members of warrior clans wearing animal hides in battle. When the 'berserker-fury' was upon them, warriors were thought of as were-bears or werewolves, neither fully human nor fully animal but merging the two (Pollington 2001). One who could transform in this way was said to be *hamrammr*, 'shape-strong'. Wolf and Bear are obvious totems for warriors, both having strong protective instincts and, when required, great stamina, strength and aggression coupled with considerable intelligence. My own working with spirit Wolves thus seems to be part of a widespread tradition spanning at least 12,000 years and much of the northern hemisphere.

The idea of shape-shifting is inextricably linked with that of wolves as ancestors. We have seen how the Quileute regard themselves as descendants of shape-shifting wolves and speculated on the possible presence of folk of similar descent in Britain. In North America, several other tribes, including the Aleuts, a number of Inuit peoples and the Ojibwas maintained descent from wolves. Turkic peoples, including the Kazakhs, Uygyrs and Uzbeks, regard the grey wolf as the mother of all Turks. Many Mongolians trace their descent from Ghengis Khan, himself descended from wolves, the name of his tribe being Borjigin, 'blue wolf'. The Evenk and Chukchi peoples of Siberia both regarded wolves as shape-shifting humans, while other Siberian tribes maintained their descent from bears (Schlesier 2013: 32). Given what we have seen, it seems reasonable to conclude that our North European ancestors held similar beliefs.

Evidence of a spiritual connection with wolves and other

canines is found in Celtic contexts. One famous example is the wolf who stands beside the antlered 'shaman' figure on the Gundestrup cauldron. Dogs accompany various deities including the Romano-British God, Nodens, whose healing sanctuary was at Lydney, in Gloucestershire. A wolf and bear accompany a horned figure on a stone carving from Meigle in Perthshire, Scotland. A horned, bearded figure carved on the 9th century CE stone Market Cross in Kells, County Meath, Ireland, is flanked by a wolf and a dog.

Wolves, then, may come to us as ancestors, as tribal or clan totems, as guides to both the living and the dead, as alter-egos for shape-shifting deities, warriors, teachers, healers or spirit-workers such as those commonly referred to by the Siberian Evenk term 'shaman'. The animist world view, of course, recognises our kinship not just with animals, but also with non-animate creatures such as trees, rocks or lightning. In an objective sense, this is true, since we all consist of atoms having their origins in the Big Bang. We truly are stardust. Narrowing down that sense of kinship to a single species, however, enables us to focus more clearly on a specific relationship within the universal web of being we inhabit. This allows for the creation of focused ceremonial engagements that enhance that personal relationship, enabling us to utilise it for healing, protection, growth, understanding and community. I may know philosophically that we are one with the universe, but I know instinctively, intuitively and cell-deep that I am Wolf.

This answers the question posed earlier as to where my current spiritual link with Wolf comes from. I am Wolf. Wolf is me. My Wolf-brother was certainly with me before I first became aware of him in that sweat lodge 20 years ago. I have spent the intervening years learning to work with him consciously, and with the spirits of our pack who came with the wolf-skin cloak. We must be doing something right as a second wolf-skin cloak, of a similar age to the first, but in even better condition, has come to us since. Like the first, it also consists of the trimmed down hides of six wolves. I also have a complete hide of a single wolf, complete with head, legs and tail, so I now sleep with 13 wolves on my bed. They are excellent company.

To bring one part of my journey full circle, a few months ago I had the opportunity to drum and sing again with my brothers and sisters of the Quileute tribe. The ceremony had changed from ten years ago, the songs sung now being entirely local, replacing the cowboy songs and even pop songs that had featured previously. Of equal significance was the return of masked dancers embodying spirit beings, including Wolf. Their presence marks another stage in the recent resurgence of the tribe. There were half a dozen masked dancers the night I was there, one a boy about eight years of age. I have seldom seen such clear focus on the face of a child. We drummers formed up in a group to one side of the dance circle. During the dances, we provided accompaniment with drums and voices. After each dance, the masked dancers filed out from the circle and crouched down on the floor in the middle of the drummers. Our role then was to lean in towards them and to drum fast and loud, drumming energy into the dancers for the next dance. It was a powerful night.

Since my initial encounter with the Wolf in the sweat lodge, we have journeyed far together. Without him, I doubt I would ever have gone to America, let alone discovered my kinship with the Quileute and their neighbours, the Makah. The presence of the Wolf spirit in my life has had a profound effect on many aspects of my spirituality, not least by opening up the ability to shape-shift. Without the Wolf connection, I doubt I would have met the God Woden on a Wiltshire hilltop at dusk. I feel a strong kinship with physical wolves, too, and keep an eye on their fate around the world. Despite their intelligence and the key role they play in eco-systems, they remain feared, misunderstood and, as a result, are often persecuted and killed. I am a passionate supporter of the reintroduction of wild wolves into Britain. My relationship with other animals has changed too. I continue to eat meat. I have developed a greater understanding and appreciation of deer, the natural prey species of my Wolf self. I connect with Bear spirit through one of my sons who has Bear magic. My relationship with the rest of nature has changed too. I feel much more comfortable in woodlands on moonless nights. My night vision seems to have improved.

Having begun with an ancient verse from the *Rig Veda*, it seems appropriate to close with a modern one. Another result of being Wolf is the inspiration it brings. In the British Druid tradition, we call inspiration *awen* and view it as a powerful, spiritual force that flows through all of creation (Shallcrass 2011a). Wolf inspired me to write a song that invokes animal spirits of the four quarters in my native tradition. In the first verse, a Stag of seven tines bells in the west, quarter of sunset and autumn. A Brown Bull guards the north, quarter of darkness and wintertime. A golden Eagle resides in the east, quarter of sunrise and of spring. And then there's the south, region of fire and summer's heat:

> *I am the lord of the wildwood,*
> *my brother wolves around me stand.*
> *Our cry rings out beneath the full moon's light*
> *and echoes far across the land.*
> *We have been here since time's beginning,*
> *howling our passions to the moon,*
> *and now the time is fast returning,*
> *when all will hear our sacred rune.*
> Lord of the Wildwood, by Greywolf.[3]

I have no direct evidence of wolf ancestry in my bloodline. Absence of evidence is not, though, evidence of absence. In the British Druid Order, we speak of ancestors of blood and of spirit (Shallcrass 2011b). Those of blood are, of course, our direct bloodline. Those of spirit are those who have walked similar spirit paths to us and with whom we therefore feel a kinship that may, in some cases, be stronger than that we have for ancestors of blood. Along my own line of spiritual ancestry, and perhaps of blood ancestry too, I'm sure there were those who recognised their own descent from shape-shifting wolves, who wore wolf pelts, who drummed and chanted and howled at the moon just as I do.

Bibliography

Author unknown c.1500-1200 BCE. 'Hymn XIV, To Yama, Hindu God of the Underworld and Guardian of the South' in *The Rig Veda* quoted in Shallcrass, Philip 2011. 'Honouring Our Ancestors', in *Bardic Course Booklet* 10, British Druid Order, Devizes.

Brown, Dorcas, R. and Anthony, David, W. 2012. *Midwinter Dog Sacrifices and Warrior Initiations in the Late Bronze Age at the Site of Krasnosamarskoe, Russia.* Presented at the Roots of Europe – Language, Culture, and Migrations Conference December 12-14, 2012, University of Copenhagen. Hartwick College, New York.

Byock, Jesse 1998. *The Saga of King Hrolf Kraki.* Penguin, London.

Frachtenberg, L. J. 1921, 'The Ceremonial Societies of the Quileute Indians', in *American Anthropologist*, vol. 23, no. 3, pp. 320-352.

Davies, Sioned (trans.), 2007. *The Mabinogion.* Oxford University Press. See especially pages 52-4 for the transformations of Gwydion and Gilvaethwy.

Hutton, Ronald 2013. *Pagan Britain*, pp. 192-3. Yale University Press, New Haven: 192-3 and page 3 in www.english-heritage.org.uk/publications/iha-burnt-mounds/burnt-mounds.pdf accessed 17/02/2015.

O'hOgain, Daithi 1990. *Myth, Legend & Romance: An Encyclopaedia of the Irish Folk Tradition*, p. 136. Ryan Publishing.

Pollington, Stephen 2001. *The English Warrior From Earliest Times Till 1066*, pp. 85-88. Anglo-Saxon Books.

Schlesier, Karl, H. 2013 (1987). *The Wolves of Heaven: Cheyenne Shamanism, Ceremonies, and Prehistoric Origins*, CreateSpace Independent Publishing Platform, New York.

Shallcrass, Philip 2000. *Druidry: A Practical and Inspirational Guide*: 7. Piatkus, London.

Shallcrass, Philip 2011a. 'Awen: The Holy Spirit of Druidry' in *Bardic Course Booklet 5*. British Druid Order, Devizes.

Shallcrass, Philip 2011b. 'Honouring Our Ancestors' in *Bardic Course Booklet 10*. British Druid Order, Devizes.

Ancestors and Place: Seidr and Other Ways of Knowing

By Jenny Blain

And far abune the Angus straths I saw the wild geese flee,
A lang, lang skein o beatin wings wi their heids towards the sea.
(Jacob 1915)

Introduction: 'Where we are'

One of the key impulses for many people is to know 'where we are'. That is not only to see on a map where we're now physically located, but to have a sense of the history, the changes, the landscape and vegetation of the place where we now are, and where we were, and where we have come from. In this chapter I intend to explore some ideas coming from my own perceptions of place, movement, and time, and to look into how the spiritual ways of 'seidr' might give some insight to an understanding of the interaction of place and human-person, and how in turn relationships with wights and ancestors form part of how seidr is worked and what can be thus achieved.

I live, now, in what was the equivalent of a Baltic Port though on the other side of the North Sea. Look at a map, and think about the ways that people travelled and connected, 1,000, 2,000, 3,000 years ago. Dundee, in Scotland, was a small town with a protected harbour, and with a straight sail into the Baltic. Indeed, I've heard it said that as little as 300 years ago, it was faster to go to Norway than to Edinburgh. I think that this relates to the mostly land journey to Edinburgh, including a ferry across the river Tay, a trek by horse or carriage through Fife, and then either a problematic ferry, less sheltered than that over the Tay and with a legendary history of accidents, or a long detour followed by a less difficult ferry and a long road back; several days longer than the three days of sailing east. Or, faster, the journey by ship from the port of Dundee to that of Leith, needing to judge the tides well, but dependent more than that on the shipping routes and so, on simply where the ships went to from Dundee – which was not necessarily Edinburgh. The comparison is with today's airline flights, and where they go from and to.

That is a very long way of saying that Dundee, in Scotland, where I live and also where I grew up, has a history that connects to Scandinavia and to the Baltic, rather more than even to some parts of Scotland: and also that before the development of today's roads, railways, and bridges, water was a way of connecting people, rather than a barrier between them.

I left Dundee in my 20s and returned in 2013. In between, I lived in Edinburgh, in Newfoundland briefly, in Halifax, Nova Scotia for many years, in the south of England for a few scant months and then in the Sheffield area of England for more than a decade. In all of these, the landscape was important and it was needful to me to in some sense 'know' the place, 'know' the landscape, in order to have a relationship with that place and, essentially, to 'know' who I was at that time. This included 'knowing' the human people who had been on that landscape, and likewise the other-than-human people there then and now, the changing fauna of the region and the changing spirits of these people. In Nova Scotia this was most evident to me through the legends of Kluskap, who might be God or trickster by turn within the Mi'kmaq stories that I met there. I was privileged, one summer night on a campsite, to see something that might be Kluskap striding through the autumn mists and hear his birds, particularly the loons, calling on the waters there.

When I returned to the United Kingdom, this attempt to 'know' the land involved me in exploring meanings of sacred sites, moving from Avebury (near where I lived for several months on my return) and others, including Stonehenge and Stanton Drew in the south of England, to places in Derbyshire and Yorkshire around Sheffield and further north. This included Thornborough Henges, where traces of past meeting places and possible religious performance coexisted with today's uses in farming and walking, as a place of brown hares and of recent annual Beltane celebrations. Some of this pursuit generated academic work, in part with a research colleague, resulting in a series of papers and the book *Sacred Sites, Contested Rites/Rights.* (Blain & Wallis 2007) It also resulted in more personal 'journey' essays, as I suppose this one is, such as my chapter in *The Wanton Green.* (MacLellan and Cross 2012) That related to the landscapes of the Scottish lowlands, to my ancestors within these lands and to the flight of the wild geese from seashore to hill and farmland, the great skeins with the constant communication of their cries as they fly.

Throughout, though, I have been pursuing ideas of seidr – the Icelandic spelling is Seiðr or in modern Icelandic Seiður, sometimes Anglicised as Seidhr – as part of the Heathen spirituality I've been learning for several decades. This is partially described in some of the Sagas, hinted at in Eddic poetry, and seems to be connected to consciousness, to ways of knowing and to ways of instituting some kind of change in 'what is', by an association between the practitioner and other beings in the place where she or he is. Present-day writings on seidr range from the academic, examples being Clive Tolley (2009) on the occurrences in the sagas and Neil Price (2001) on archaeological evidence, to those of practitioners such as Diana Paxson (2008), Johnson and Wallis (2005), 'Runic John' (2004, 2013) and Gerrard (2011). In anthropological fieldwork, I observed present-day constructions of seidr and took part in these, and as a practicing Heathen developed seidr work together with a small group in Nova Scotia where I then was, while searching the Sagas and other writings for background for both purposes. One result was my 2002 book, *Nine Worlds of Seid-Magic,* attempting an auto-ethnographic understanding of some forms of seidr being developed today.

Later results have included speculations on using seidr techniques to 'know' – or rather to gain insights into – pasts not only from the pre-Christian period, but also from much later times, applying this, therefore, to my other pre-occupation, my own ancestors and their lives and being within landscapes of Lowland Scotland.

Knowing the past is difficult and fraught with many problems. We cannot step into their shoes. The past is indeed 'another country' or rather many countries, and things are/were indeed done 'differently' there. Even in returning to my own landscape of birth, in Dundee and Angus, much has changed not only in the demolition and construction (and further demolition and construction, in very short spaces of time) of buildings, but also in what people do, even how they think of themselves in relation to 'God' and place, and in the language spoken around me and hence the ways of expressing and transmitting knowledge encapsulated there.

> *Whit's deefferent then? Whaur's the chynges frae the leid o fowks when ye wis a wee lass in an industrial toun? Weel, it's no that eevident, no straught tae speir or tae tell. Ane thing is oan the bus gaein intae toun there's nae the gab aboot Goad or the Kirk but jist aboot the wey things fa oot, an whit gaes on in ilka place. An thar's a but nane o yon weavers, no sae mony loons taken prenticeships, no sae mony lasses gaein tae the factories the noo.*

Times change and we move on. The weaving factories and the spinning mills that fuelled their output are converted to flats, or sometimes museums, and many of the lasses are at university. My hometown is at once 'upskilling' and becoming a town noted for design, while also remaining one of the poorest areas of Scotland and, indeed, the UK, with generation gaps and social class rifts even within quite small housing districts.

But to my tale; knowing pasts, Seiðr and landscapes. Seiðr is based in the relationship between human and what Graham Harvey (2005, 2012) terms other-than-human persons. There is a sense here of being interdependent with others – this meant in a positive way, in that we each are embedded within networks of being, each a small part of both place and time. So, if I want to create something in my part of the world, I cannot compel other people to help, but have to ask. If I want birds to come into my garden, I put out bird feeders, plant things I think will assist them, and hope. My agency relates to what I do, not what they do. In this I'm seeing Seiðr as a means of being within a Heathen worldview, closely related to the shamanic or shamanistic practices and worldviews of the north of Eurasia, perhaps closest to Sámi understandings and indeed in part possibly derived from these (Dubois 1999).

Heathenry is not defined strictly by either its practices or its beliefs. Rather, it can be seen as collections of beliefs and practices that centre on a shared set of cosmological concepts, within sets of relationships of beings. These are described in Icelandic literature, particularly in the cosmogonic poems of the Poetic Edda, from which adherents derive their own under-standings. Indeed, all Heathenry today owes a great debt to this literature. Today's Heathens engage with the Poetic Edda as a source rich in inspirational material. The first poem, Völuspá or the speaking of the Seeress, has the speaker, 'remember(ing) very early', and might be viewed as a starting point not only cosmo-logically, but also for remembering and re-deploying ancient Norse myth as lore or knowledge relevant to today. Larrington (1993) links the Hávamál, the second and longest poem of the Poetic Edda, to 'Wisdom Poetry' elsewhere, pointing to specific features including complexity and progression from simple maxims for everyday life (don't get drunk, be a good guest in the mead-hall, and so on) to the training of a 'prince' to the rather more esoteric mysteries of the rune verses. Many Heathens in the UK and elsewhere have combed Hávamál for an idea of how a

Heathen community, that is one looking to the old Gods and the understandings of much of the north of Europe (notably Iceland), should be constructed. They have looked to others of the Eddic poems for understandings of the relationships of deities and human people and ways in which everyday and mystical events can relate to each other, the ways that worlds are interdependent. That's where I'll begin.

Heathen cosmology

At the centre of Heathenry is the concept of the world tree, Yggdrasil, the 'steed of Yggr' or Odin; and the pool of Wyrd at its foot, tended by three women, the Norns who spin or otherwise craft fate or *Wyrd* for individuals or communities. Wyrd is not a simple determinism, but could be seen more as potential for people to create their lives, together with obligations on them; people are part of the shaping of their own Wyrd, as their past actions become part of who they are and part of what connects them to others. Nine worlds variously described in poetry have their being, conceptually, on the branches of the tree, or possibly below its roots; each has its own 'people', and the human world, Midgard, is shared with many other *wights* (from the Old English word *wiht*, a sentient being). A general interpretation of the upper world, Asgard, is the abode of Gods, while Midgard is 'middle-earth', inhabited by humans, and lower worlds are those of the dark-elves and of Hel, the place of ancestors. Also on the branches of the tree, however, are the worlds of the light-elves (often seen as a further 'upper world' realm), those of the Jotnar (Etins or giants) and the Vanir, and more distant and less comprehensible, the worlds of fire and ice from which creation began. This is a complex pattern, and there are different ways to name 'worlds'; it is a conceptual rather than a physical map. The concept of the world tree or central pillar connecting many worlds allies with those of the shamanic cosmologies of northern Eurasia. Some of the deities of

Heathenry likewise have parallels in Eastern European mythologies or observations.

How this is interpreted and used to structure today's Heathenry varies, however, from attempting to 'reconstruct' practices to attempting to derive and adapt understanding and worldview. Many Heathens use the word 'reconstructionist' of themselves, but others dislike this as it gives the impression that they are trying to be 'the same' as in 'the past' (whatever that is). Those I'm terming shamanic or shamanistic – maybe animic, in the sense in which Graham Harvey uses the term, is a stronger description – find a basis for understanding in the relationships between categories or orders of beings, be these humans, Gods, wights, deer, dragonflies, diving beetles. Those who practice a more 'Gods-centred' Heathenry in general appear to focus on how to honour the deities, often drawing boundaries around sets of deities who are 'Heathen' and others seen as from elsewhere, other cultures. Those who work with the land, though, may take a more inclusive view of both Gods and ancestors – those Heathens I know tend to agree that boundaries around Heathenry are very fuzzy, that Gods do what they will, associate with whom they will, and that those who find themselves drawn to Heathenry and Heathen understandings are Heathen, whatever their ancestries or ethnicities.

Ancestors, though, do matter, very greatly, but can be understood as people in the land and the stories of place – that is, not only physical 'ancestors' but those who have been related to where we are now, and those who have given us the knowledge, tools, ways of being that we now use in both mundane and spiritual lives. So, the 'ancestors' I honour in ritual include people from around the world, but notably those such as the unknown Saga writers, and much closer to home the Angus poet Violet Jacob, with whose words on the Wild Geese I grew up. The geese she wrote of are themselves ancestors to some of those who fly, today, over my garden and the nearby woodland, from their winter roosts by the shores of sea and Tay to the farmlands where they forage, returning each night and calling to each other, their voices trailing on the air.

Ancestors and landwights

In looking into animist Heathenry, I find a focus on where people are and how they interact with other people – that is both human and non-human people, and in pasts as well as the present. Quite near the beginning of my anthropological fieldwork on Heathenry and its meanings and practices I interviewed Jörmundur Ingi Hansen, then the leader of the Ásatrúarfélagið in Iceland. He discussed how in the Icelandic writings, 'the Gods' were not necessarily the main focus for many people. Some individuals of course were goðar (priest/esses) for particular Gods, usually referred to in the Sagas as 'friends' of Thor or Freyr or Freyja or Odinn. The Althing, the old parliament, opened with a request to the Gods to bless the work, but the core, he says, was the relationship with landwights.

> ...and we get this feeling more and more, that ah, that the real core of Ásatrú is the landwights. Ah, there is no good, there is no good, ah, definition of landwights anywhere, that what they actually are, except that they are spirits and ah, and they in some way control the safety of the land, the fertility of the land, and so on. The ah, friend of mine, who is a sort of mystic, and was in India for a long time, he claims that he knows exactly what a landwight is, ah, and until I get a better one, this is the one I will stick to. He says, a landwight is a spirit, or a soul if you like, who uses a land for a body, instead of a biological body. And so, the landwight would be connected ah, to ah, to a special spot, and, and this is usually, when you start thinking of it, this is usually the idea in Iceland, that the landwights are tied to a spot in the landscape, to a huge rock, to a mountain, or to a specially

beautiful place. (Interview 1998)

The understanding from Jörmundur is interesting on many levels, not least in that it makes a connection with other spiritualities. This was continued throughout his discussion. It is also a component of British Heathenry, as I have found it, today – the idea that other spiritualities, particularly those from northern Eurasia and from some versions of Hinduism, give clues to Heathenry and what it might have developed into (had Christianity not intervened). These comments also may give another way to think about landscapes and places within these. Much Pagan discourse holds that 'all land is sacred', following some indigenous understanding, whereas Christianity appears to hold that sacredness is an attribute conferred on place or landscape by human people or by a particular event or happening, so that a place can be consecrated or deconsecrated by human people. The idea of landwights being attached to particular places gives an ability for all land to be sacred, in the sense that it is its own thing and to be engaged with and respected, but that there are some places where this sacredness becomes focused so it is easier for human people to appreciate this. In this discourse, landwights are everywhere – some are more manifest, more able to communicate with other communities.

And there are not only landwights, but also housewights attached to buildings, riverwights, and various others. Within an animist (or animic) approach, one can see all places as populated with other-than-human (other than fox, other than dragonfly) people, of whom some are more communicative than others; which leads to ideas of human people (and other-than-human people) undertaking seidr or shamanic Heathen practice.

Heathenry differs from Wicca and some other forms of Paganism today, in there is an understanding that some people, not all, will be practitioners of magical or seidr work, to various degrees. Seidr work is specialised, taught, learned through experience and indeed apprenticeship, just as playing a musical instrument, farming, or creating art through woodworking are specialised and learned. Therefore, many Heathens do not themselves work seidr, but within the UK at least, increasingly respect those who do and see themselves as living within a landscape where 'seidr magic' is at least possible, a re-enchanted landscape where wights and ancestors may be found and Gods might walk, though not all humans will play attention to these, and those that do, not all of the time. While many Heathens do not see themselves as 'magic workers' they see magic as a relational component of what surrounds them, and so we come to the accounts of seidr.

Seidr in Heathenry today and in past accounts

What we, today, know about seidr in the past comes from those sources that have survived, and these were written (or written down) after 'conversion' so that their analysis is tricky. They are not simply accounts of what happened, but accounts told for the purpose of the storytelling. Best known, and most detailed, is the story told in the Saga of Eirik the Red. A farm in Greenland has fallen on hard times and a famous seeress, the last of nine 'sisters', is invited to the farmstead to tell what may be. This is one of the more detailed descriptions of any personage in the Sagas; her clothing and shoes, her staff and cloak, are detailed. She wears a hood of lambskin lined with catskin, and has white catskin gloves. Her gown is girdled with a belt of touchwood, from which hangs a bag to hold magical items. Her cloak is blue, fastened with straps and adorned with stones, and stones stud the head of her staff. Her calfskin shoes are tied with thick laces, with tin buttons on their ends. She is asked to predict the progress of the community; she eats a meal including a porridge made from goat's milk or colostrum and of the hearts of the farm animals, and the next day a 'high seat' is made ready for her, where she will sit to foretell. She engages in ritual practices to make *seiðr*, and these require a special song to be sung to call or bind 'the powers' or spirits, in order that she may gain their knowledge. To do this, she sits on a raised platform (*seiðhjallr*), on a cushion stuffed with hen's feathers, to make her predictions, but then a problem arises. This quoted description is from a recent translation:

> Later the following day she was provided with things she required to carry out her magic rites. She asked for women who knew the chants required for carrying out magic rites, which are called ward songs (*Varðlokur*). But such women were not to be found. Then the people of the household were asked if there was anyone with such knowledge.
>
> Gudrid answered, 'I have neither magical powers nor the gift of prophecy, but in Iceland my foster-mother, Halldis, taught me chants she called ward songs.'
>
> [After some persuasion] the women formed a warding ring around the platform raised for sorcery, with Thorbjorg perched atop it. Gudrid spoke the chant so well and so beautifully that people there said they had never heard anyone recite in a fairer voice.
>
> The seeress thanked her for her chant. She said many spirits had been attracted who thought the chant fair to hear – 'though earlier they wished to turn their backs on us and refused to do our bidding. Many things are now clear to me which were earlier concealed from both me and others.' (*Eiríks saga rauða*, trans. Kunz 2000: 658)

The seeress then spoke 'futures' for the community as a whole, predicting that the farm would survive, and for individuals within it, notably a famous life for Guðríðr who sang for her. The account of Þorbjörg has formed a basis, along with other descriptions, for today's practice of *oracular seiðr*, also known as *high-seat seiðr* or spae-working, reconstructed in different ways by groups focusing on different points in the account. There can be no surety that this particular episode happened as indicated, or indeed even happened at all.[1] The account and the writing of the Saga date from at least 200 years after the described incident, and are told as background and introduction for the heroine, Guðríðr, whose story runs throughout the Saga. However, the details in this account may indicate much about how seeresses were thought of, by people claiming to be their descendants or inheritors and retaining stories of their practice, including their costume, their way of life, and how they might be regarded in time of crisis; and how they were expected to behave and what they would need to talk with the spirits.

In particular, it presents seidr as something positive under-taken to gain knowledge and as community practice, indeed requiring the communities involved to take part. The account explicitly calls what the seeress does 'seidr', saying that she requires 'að fremja seiðinn', that is 'to make the seidr' in order to have the knowledge she needs, which she cannot gain by other means. However, it may be that she is doing more than 'seeing', but also actively shaping these futures by speaking them, with the cooperation of the 'spirits' that have been drawn to help by the chanting of Guðríðr and the other women.

I first met seidr, many years ago and in North America, as attempted reconstruction based in that Greenland seeing, bringing in also the Völuspá verses of question and answer, and the refrain from the seeress of, 'Would you know more, or what?' This was a powerful experience and subsequent seidr events and experiments remained similarly powerful. Some of these are detailed by me elsewhere (Blain 2002, 2005, 2012). This version of 'oracular seidr' focuses on what appears key in the various accounts, the raised seat and the singing, with some emphasis also on the third item, the staff of the seeress.

These elements occur in other mentions of seidr throughout

the sagas, not always together, and so have been adopted by practitioners today, in attempts to develop seidr as a means to connect with the workings of Wyrd to effect some kind of change, whether that be a change in knowledge, in health of an individual or community or indeed of the land itself, or some other kind of change such as conveying protection on a person or place or to create the circumstances to enable an individual to fulfil their potential.

It is important, though, to recognise the ambiguity with which seidr practice and its practitioners were viewed within saga accounts, some of which have tinged today's seid also. Many accounts are of seid-magic performed against the hero of the saga, with only a few being presented as definitively positive – the above account of the Greenland seeress and the story in the Book of Settlements of Thurid the Sound-filler who sings fish into the bays to help the human people back to prosperity, being two. There are, therefore, mentions of seeing-women being treated with respect, as specialists whose work is necessary for the community, in both Family Sagas of Icelanders, and the 'Legendary Sagas'. An example of the latter is the seeress Heið of Hrólfs saga Kraka, of whom Morris (1991: 45) says:

> King Frodi asked her to make use of her talents, prepared a feast for her, and set her on platform for her spell-making. She then opened her mouth, yawned, cast a spell and chanted a verse.

Likewise, Þórdís the seeress of Kormáks saga and of Vatnsdæla saga was 'held in great esteem and knew many things', and the hill behind her dwelling was named after her Spákonufell, the mountain of the seeress. In Vatnsdæla she uses her power to resolve a dispute in court, turning to magical means, when a culprit will not accept that he is in the wrong, to force him to make restitution, and this is approved by the community: yet in the Saga of Kormak the Skald her offer of magical assistance is rejected by the hero. There are also ambiguous elements in the 'seeing' of Heið, mentioned above, who is respected and feasted, but who is compelled through the seidr state to reveal what she does not want to.

Some other accounts project seidr as purely negative, for instance that of the seer Kotkel and his family in Laxdaela Saga; and in many instances, even that of the Greenland Seeress Þorbjörg, the one who 'makes seidr' is shown as separate from the community, living apart, being called in to assist, though respected and potentially holding a high position, but with that ambiguity still present. And, while most of the seid workers described are women, when men are spoken of as working seidr they are generally doing so against the protagonist of whichever story is being told. This is tied in with the descriptions of seid-men as 'ergi', possibly crossing gender boundaries as the 'unmanly man' (Meulengracht Sørenson 1983) even in performing seidr if this was seen to be something in which women were specialists, and with apparent persecution of seid-men described in the early histories of Norway (see e.g. Blain 2002 for more on this).

Today, 'oracular seidr' is undertaken by women and men, and has developed its own sets of songs to call the 'spirits' and to assist the creation of whatever change is sought. This can take place within an elaborate ritual structure, or within a far simpler framework though based in the cosmological concepts of the tree Yggdrasil and the pool of Wyrd at its foot. The idea is that Yggdrasil as World Tree provides a ladder or even road to connect the worlds of Gods, humans, ancestors and other beings, and that Wyrd affects all. Human people have their Wyrd, goldfinches or hedgehogs have their Wyrd, the Gods have their Wyrd and these are neither deterministic nor separate. To return to an image from the start of this chapter, I interact with the other-than-human wights in my garden by the kinds of planting that I do, by putting out bird feeders, and so forth, and in doing this my own trajectory intersects with those of the goldfinches and robins that may come. Equally, the seid-worker sets up her or his spiritual 'garden' in ways that may attract those spirits that wish to come; she will form strong alliances with some, casual acquaintances with others, and those who come will have their own agendas that they wish to pursue.

The oracular seidr ritual, in its most elaborate form, includes the formation of a protected space and invocation of the deities who themselves are said to make seidr, Freyja and Odin, using poetry drawn from or inspired by Poetic Edda verses. This done, a set of songs are used to call to spirits and to create a shared understanding among those present, and a guided meditation undertaken to move all present from their own known landscapes to be conceptually at the foot of the tree Yggdrasil. This then goes further, through elaborate sets of imagery drawn from the mythology of Northern Europe, circling around and through the worlds on Yggdrasil to the gate to the realm of the ancestors. Here the 'pathworking' ceases, the people wait at the gate and only the seer, on a high seat or raised platform, will go further, assisted by song – now much reliant on a steady beat – into the land of the dead where lies Hela's hall. When the seer indicates that she or he is 'there' then a session of questions and answers begins, facilitated by a seidr guide who acts as an inter-mediary, inviting audience participants to ask their questions of the seer who can then, in a deep altered consciousness, attempt to 'see' assisted by whatever helper beings come to her, and speak what is seen. The seer may, as need requires, 'go' elsewhere, within Hel's realm, or into other landscapes (even in one account to another planet) to gain answers. The spirits that assist may be deities, may be ancestors whether her own or those of the querant, may be other beings in the land, but include in the key role of protector her own fylgja, 'follower' or 'fetch', usually presenting as an animal.

Speaking from the high seat, in a deep trance, is not easy; indeed this may be one of the most difficult elements in the oracular trance. Two factors intervene: the physical requirement to make mouth and tongue work, and the modern 'conditioning', as seidkona Diana Paxson has described it, that causes us to doubt and to revert to what is considered 'reality', even to edit what is spoken and tend to pull the practitioner back from the altered consciousness that they need to maintain for the seidr. The elaborate ritual has been designed to assist the maintenance of this state, through a different 'conditioning' that enables everyday concerns and our 'rational' modern analysis to be set aside, but also is designed for an audience with little familiarity with the mythology of the North or even the concepts of Yggdrasil and Wyrd.

However, the elaborate ritual is only one way to make seidr. It does, though, give a very thorough training in what may be needed, including the ability to relate to song as a means of altering consciousness, and to keep a focus within the cosmology and imagery of the North. It also gives an awareness of seidr as something that links the Wyrds of those involved with a particular session at a particular time and place, and gives protection when the seidworker encounters something that is difficult or even dangerous; and it emphasises the discipline of working with one's own fylgja and other helper spirits, becoming familiar with these so that trust is developed. As an example here, unwanted spirit possession has been encountered and dealt with, as with one seidman's unpleasant experience with an ancestor of his querant, which entered his body and proved to be 'not a pleasant of good wight'. (For details of this see Blain 2002: 64. Note that this is different from the 'deity possession' that may at times be sought as part of seidr practice.) This seer's helper spirits told him how to expel the wight. Different practitioners develop their own songs and relate to their own helper beings, as key to their practice, and in doing so have drawn on various forms of 'shamanic' involvement elsewhere, both traditional and 'urban'.

So if the key features of seidr are the song, raised platform and staff, and the involvement of other-than-human beings, the final section of this chapter will ask some questions about these beings, how they relate to human practitioners, and how they include ancestors.

Seidr, wights and ancestors

In the elaborate oracular seidr described above, other-than-human beings are called through invocation and song. These are in particular the deities who perform seidr, other Gods, and various wights including land spirits and ancestors. Others may be honoured in song, beings such as the Mörnir who have been described by practitioner Raudhild as female etins or giants, very ancient, those who are indicated in that verse from Völuspa mentioned earlier where the Völva, the great seeress says, 'I born of giants remember very early...'[2] Raudhild has given me an account of her initiation by these cave-dwelling beings, paralleling trance experiences narrated by shamans elsewhere (in Blain 2002).

Seidworkers today place great emphasis on the need for helper spirits and the roles of these within any form of seidr, be this 'oracular' seidr for a community, or seidr performed for healing or protection, or to learn about a place and its history or for 'de-ghosting'. The story of the seer, above, told by his helper spirits how to expel a wight from his body is a case in point. These spirits include, centrally, the fylgja or 'follower', but there may be many others, who become important in other areas of life; one seidkona has spoken of being instructed in her cooking by great-aunts who may approve or sometimes question what she is doing. Those who 'walk with' seidworkers may include ancestors of many kinds – recent 'known' relatives, often female, may enable seeing; or seeing, in the form of deliberate dreaming or of 'sitting out for wisdom' may be undertaken in quest for who ancestors were. Ancestors of other kinds, such as those who lived within the practitioner's landscape, may also form part of the seidr, or once again sitting out may be a way of attempting to 'know' them – particularly for people undertaking meditation at sacred sites.

Sitting out, or *útiseta* comes also from the old literature. It typically involved sitting on a gravemound or at a crossroads, though in the form of 'going under the cloak' it could be done wherever one was, to gain knowledge or understanding of what was or had been, or to see possible futures. Unlike today's oracular seidr ritual it is a solitary practice though in the literature could be undertaken on behalf of a community, as in the story of the conversion of Iceland where the Lawspeaker goes 'under the cloak' for a day and a night, emerging to tell what he has learned. Both forms implied or required a distancing of oneself from the other human members of the community, so that the 'sitter' was not to be disturbed, and according to Aðalsteinsson (1978) their name should not be mentioned while they undertook this task.

Sitting out for wisdom, in today's work, returns me to the ideas of 'knowing the past' with which I began this chapter. Today the crossroads or gravemound might be replaced by a historic place, a graveyard, a prehistoric site. Knowing of this sort involves communication: between the seer or seeker and what beings they meet, and again between the seer and those on whose behalf they are working. What is the communication, and with whom?

In that account of seidr from Eiriks Saga, several points seem pertinent. Firstly, the spirits are termed, in the saga, 'náttúrur', which is not an Icelandic word with an exact translation, but a word derived from Latin and implying 'nature spirits'. Who were the spirits or powers called by Guðríðr's song? It seems that the seidkona needed to gain knowledge of the place to which she had been called; she could not make her seidr right away, but ate a meal specially prepared, including meat from the hearts of the various types of animals on the farm – this is a situation where the people did not know if the farm could survive. Then she slept, and only the next day did she sit upon her raised platform with its cushions. There seems to me a sense here that she had to know the farm, and its beings, in some form. And this is double-edged. She seemingly needed to learn the landscape through taking into herself something of the beings who inhabited this space, the animals (sheep, geese, possibly cattle) who were present and who interacted every day with the humans and with the wights of the farm; but the giving of their hearts in a meal to her was, from a farmstead that faced famine, a very major sacrifice. The giving and preparing of her meal – let's not forget that these animals were slaughtered, butchered and their hearts cooked by the farm people, however they may have viewed this – represented an offering from the farm to the old Gods, and may have appeared to them as a major giving up of part of their own health, wealth, and indeed their survival chances. The meal therefore seems part of the ritualised structure of the seidr.

Secondly, the *dealing with the spirits* holds an immediacy – the people in the Greenland farm knew what these spirits were, and quite possibly themselves made offerings to them, or at least those who were not Christian may have done so. In folklore, every farm has its nature spirits, its wights (or nissen) with whom the farm people work, and have their traditions derived from those who have previously worked this land – although the Greenland farm was a new settlement and therefore may have been developing its own traditions of offering, based on those used previously in Iceland, Ireland and Scotland, and Scandinavia, the lands from which its human people came and where their ancestors lay.

Then, there is a sense of these ancestors, whether of the Greenland farm people or of today's seers, where they are, and how they become part of the experience of seidr or of sitting out. How were they thought of, how did they feature in the migrations of people and in their farming? Once again, there may be a clue in the interviews I conducted with Jörmundur in Iceland, who spoke of traditional farming customs and the 'ground of the ancestors', saying, 'Everywhere in Iceland, every farm had a patch of land that you could never farm on and never utilise, ah, because it was sacred ground.' According to him, ancestors were present, in the ground and in people's memories, though becoming more distant if not remembered, and he drew a parallel here with deities and landwights who might similarly fade from view if they faded from memory. Death, he said, was not something abrupt, but part of a slow process of being gradually removed from the 'world' of human people.

As said before, 'ancestors' for many Heathens include not only their recent kin, but also those of the past who have influenced them, such as the writers of the Sagas, and those who have lived on and are now within the landscapes in which we work. So, for seidworkers, ancestors can be present both in memory and within the physical place where we are. I have found differences in working seidr in most of North America and in the British Isles, not so much in ritual form as in the necessity of this form, and found these differences also in the accounts of practitioners from elsewhere in Europe. The knowledge of place, and connection with place, matters. In the US there seemed a key focus of having Gods – notably Freyja and Odin – lead the way in seidr practice. In Britain, this has seemed – to me and to others with whom I've discussed this – unnecessary, almost irrelevant unless in the sense of 'honouring' deities or asking 'protection'. Wights and ancestors are in the landscape and they enable seidr.

I have speculated that there are several possibilities here. One relates to the reluctance, understandably, of North American Heathens to be seen to 'appropriate' local land spirits, so respecting Native spiritual traditions. Where there is a history of recent extreme exploitation, sensitive practitioners take care to not add to this, but rather may restrict their practices to asking permission, rather than asking assistance, of those beings who are part of the landscape. Another possibility is that the means of relating to these may be based in land, in place, even in the seas and currents, and so dealing with spirits in California (where much of today's seidr practice involving ritual formulae was developed) is likely to be very different from that in even Nova Scotia – where I started developing my own practice. The shores of Nova Scotia are washed by the Atlantic, and on the rocks grey seals congregate in winter, and they sing with human voices.

So to conclude this on a personal note, as how it started – after returning from Nova Scotia, I lived for 14 years in Sheffield, and found that area conducive to an easier form of seidr practice, more informal than that I'd learned, and more immediate in the sense it gave of communication with those who had lived in that landscape and changed it, creating the small stone circles and cairns of the Peak District. But now I have returned to my roots in Dundee, where the landscape and cityscape call to me, where ancestral voices echo in the streets and cemeteries and in the stories of the growth of the burgh, its shipping and its trades. And my house and garden, on the edge of the city by woodland and farmland, are with within easy distance of the Angus Braes of the poem which inspired my connection to landscape, so long ago: The Wild Geese.

Bibliography

Aðalsteinsson, Jön, Hnefill 1978. *Under the Cloak*. *Acta Universitatis Upsaliensis 4*. Almqvist & Wiksell, Uppsala.

Blain, Jenny 2002. *Nine Worlds of Seid-Magic: Ecstasy and Neo-Shamanism in North European Paganism*. Routledge, London.

Blain, Jenny 2005. 'Now Many of Those Things are Shown to Me Which I Was Denied Before: Seidr, Shamanism, and Journeying, Past and Present' in *Studies in Religion/Sciences*

Religieuses 34(1) 81-98.

Blain, Jenny 2012. 'Seidr Oracles' in *Pathways in Modern Western Magic*, ed. Nevill. Drury. Concrescent, Richmond.

Blain, Jenny and Wallis, Robert, J. 2007. *Sacred Sites, Contested Rights/Rites*. Sussex Academic Press, Brighton.

Dubois, Thomas 1999. *Nordic Religions in the Viking Age*. University of Pennsylvania Press, Philadelphia.

Gerrard, Katie 2011. *Seidr: The Gate is Open*. Avalonia, London.

Harvey, Graham 2005. *Animism: Respecting the Living World*. Hurst & Company, London.

Harvey, Graham (ed.) 2013. *The Handbook of Contemporary Animism*. Acumen, Durham.

Kunz, Keneva (trans.) 2000. 'Eirik the Red's Saga' in *The Sagas of Icelanders*, eds.

Hreinsson, Viðar (ed.), Cook, R., Gunnell, T., Kunz K. and Scudder, B. Penguin Books, London: 653-674.

Jacob, Violet 1915. *Songs of Angus*. John Murray, London.

Johnson, Nathan and Wallis, Robert, J. 2005. *Galdrbok: Practical Heathen Runecraft, Shamanism and Magic*. The Wykeham Press, Winchester.

Larrington, Carolyne 1993. *A Store of Common Sense: Gnomic Theme and Style in Old Icelandic and Old English Wisdom Poetry*. Clarendon Press, Oxford.

MacLellan, Gordon and Cross, Susan (eds.) 2012. *The Wanton Green: Contemporary Pagan Writings on Place*. Mandrake, Oxford.

Meulengracht Sørenson, Preben 1983. *The Unmanly Man: Concepts of Sexual Defamation in Early Northern Society* (trans. Turville-Petre, Joan). Odense University Press, Odense.

Morris, Katherine 1991. *Sorceress or Witch? The Image of Gender in Medieval Iceland and Northern Europe*. University Press of America, Lanham.

Runic John 2004. *The Book of Seidr: The Native English and Northern European Shamanic Tradition*. Capall Bann Publishing,

Milverton.

Runic, John 2013. *Up and Down the Tree: Exploring the Nine Worlds of Yggdrasil*. Capall Bann Publishing, Milverton.

Paxson, Diana 2008. *Trance-Portation: Learning to Navigate the Inner World*. San Francisco: Red Wheel/Weiser, San Francisco.

Price, Neil 2001. *The Viking Way: Religion and War in Late Iron Age Scandinavia*. Uppsala University Press, Uppsala.

Tolley, Clive 2009. *Shamanism in Norse Myth and Magic*. 2 Vols. Academia Scientaum Fennica, Helsinki.

Wights, Ancestors, Hawks and Other Significant Others: A Heathen-Archaeologist-Falconer in Place

By Robert J Wallis

Land is exceedingly loved by each man,
if he may often enjoy its due rights
happy at home in prosperity.
(Nathan and Wallis, 2005)

Introduction

'What do you do?' – a question I dislike, as if my working life in a university defines me. 'Are you married?' and the subsequent, 'Do you have kids?' presume a heteronormative frame and a requirement to procreate when, perhaps unusually, Claire and I have lived happily together for half of our lives and children are still not top of the list. 'What are your hobbies?' suggests work and play are separate, leisure activities, a distraction or escape, when as a falconer my relationship with a hawk, a significant other and companion species, requires daily commitment, involves emotional investment, is a research subject (Wallis 2014) and bleeds into my 'spirituality' (a term that's a poor fit for what I'm getting at). Worse yet, 'What do you believe?' – the wrong question for a non-believing heathen animist whose Gods are ancestors, ancestors sometimes animals, plants occasionally allies, and allies wights. I fit in, but not quite. I'm an archaeologist, but I don't dig holes. I identify as a heathen animist (in understated lower case) but not Asatru, Odinist or Shaman. I recognise my grandmother Gladys, Gyr-falki, Woden, the plant Mugwort, the builders of Bush Barrow, yew trees and the hare Freyja caught a few days ago, within my loose approach to 'ancestors'. I'm a hedge-sitter, an out-sitter, and the ancestors are all around me and within me, part of my identity although I would not necessarily say that mine is an 'ancestral heart'. Let me attempt to explain, by starting here, in this place, just now.

At home, with wights who are allies

Thunor's Blot, known by other Pagans as Imbolc, approaches. It is minus seven outside. A hard frost stills everything and ice coats the bottom of the window panes inside the cottage.

Ice is exceeding cold, very slippery,
glistens like glass, much like a jewel,
floor frost, fair wrought, a fine sight.

It is not long after twilight and behind the alder and willow bank of the River Test there is a soft orange glow; before long Sunna will rise over the hill behind which is Knowle Clump, the Micheldever Road and the sewage works. From the opposite side of the valley, up here on Lynch Hill (lynch as in a hill near water, not lynch as in gallows), I can just see part of the dark narrow river in the gap between two Victorian houses on London Street. A little upstream, this tributary passes Town Mill Bridge where the trout gather for children to feed them bread on their way to school. A pair of azure kingfishers flashed past me there back in the summer. I was glad.

The source of the Test is a few miles further upstream, past Bere Mill and Laverstoke Mill (now the Bombay Sapphire distillery), at Ashe. The river has carved many braided strands, managed for fly-fishing, into the bright chalk of the Hampshire downs: downstream through Stockbridge which is near Danebury hillfort where I've slept in the beech-leaf litter; on to Romsey where salmon leap, though I've not yet seen it; meeting the Itchen, which flows through Winchester, where we used to live; the Itchen passing St Catherine's Hill where the Dongas and the Freeborn Tribe gathered, protested against the M3 and celebrated the land and those who came before; flowing into Southampton Water by the city where Claire and I met.

My view from the cottage is dominated by a grand old yew tree growing in a garden over the lane, its bone-like limbs coated in the darkest green through the seasons.

Yew is outwardly an unsmooth tree,
hard, fast in the earth,
a keeper of fires, roots writhing beneath,
a joy on the land.

Our cottage, number one in a row of three, was built for millworkers by the Portal family in the 1770s. The yew was ancient even then, is deep-set with long memory; of black caps, bypasses, milliners, Methodists and winning the right to protest. Though I can't see it from here, just by our front gate grows a Mugwort plant. She just appeared, not long after I had worked with, researched and written about her. I am reminded:

Remember Mugwort what you made known / what you set out in mighty revelation / 'the first' you are called oldest of herbs / you have might against three and against thirty / you have might against venom and against flying shots / you have might against the loathsome thing that fares around the land. (trans. by Wallis 2012)

The Old English *'Nine Herbs'* charm – found in the *Lacnunga* manuscript, a type of 'leechbook' or healer's manual – might give a sense of how some of our ancestors perceived a wider-than-human-world and its significant others (Haraway 2003). The charm opens by addressing the often-overlooked, but apparently mighty, Mugwort. The wort is named very deliberately, recognised as a person, and has its own significant voice.

Just then, two blackbirds clash on the path, fighting over our small patch of garden, missing out on the mealworms and peanuts while the wood pigeons glutton themselves and jackdaws, chattering dark raiders, steam in from the chimney top on Test Road where they nest every year. At the end of this road is the Silk Mill on Frog Island where the river becomes two and Claire has a small studio space with a handloom; clap-a-clap, clap-a-clap. There are dents in the wall where the industrial shuttles (now encased in wire) flew out, sometimes hitting child workers in the head. The silk is bound to the town by the river, weaves the people to the land, the earth to the sea; everything, however hackneyed it may sound, is connected.

This morning, the roof of Freyja's mews is coated in white, and her weathering lawn, and the decking and perennial borders. I need to chop the fast-growing sycamore hedge, or remove the damn thing altogether, but the hedge sparrows and tits like it so I probably won't. A single snowdrop has fought through the sleeping earth and stood proud the past few days near our front door; delicate, trembling, yet hardy and bright with life. A blackcap has just arrived from the yew tree to feed on the fat balls, a pair of blue tits follow, a dunnock is in the thorn bush; and finally a robin-friend flies in, his kin allies since the early 1990s, cocking his tail as if he owns it all.

In this place, with allies who are sometimes ancestors

Up well before dawn, hearing the bright birdsong; seeing the sun rise, the soothing river, my hawk in her weathering, the ferrets dancing in their court; Claire upstairs snoozing in bed, the wood burner warm from the night before; the bright birch, the aged yew; the perennial chalk, the ancient mounds; family I've known, those I haven't; generations of other families who came before; those who first farmed the land, cleared the woods, built industrial mills, wove silk, made roads, worshipped at St Mary's Church; loved, wept, hated and laughed; the messy mesh of life and death.

A couple of miles downstream at the hamlet of Tufton, my great aunty Phyl was born, and my great uncle Arthur further on at Wherwell (although I did not know of this family connection to the area until we moved here seven years ago). I am not and will never be a 'local', but I feel at home here, close to the rolling North Hampshire downs; set in chalk and flint, etched by rivers and rabbits, bound by hedgerows and a web of roads, crowned with hillforts and round barrows, bordered to the south by the sea, across which is Guernsey where Claire's family is from, where people half-starved during the Nazi occupation, and where similar earthen barrows and rock art were made by earlier people, 'ancestors', as those I am compelled to know elsewhere in the British Isles.

It is perhaps too easy to romanticise 'ancestors', whether recent or remote, and the land where they lived and were memorialised. The rune poem is pragmatic in its counsel:

Grave is wearisome to all who are noble,
when dear-held flesh begins to cool,
life-breath fallen, joys departed, pledges ceasing.

Writing this contribution to a book on 'the ancestral heart' in late winter and on this cold Sunday seems fitting. The land hibernates. The nights are long. Most of us spend more time indoors, keeping warm. The ghosts of the past feel closer. It is an ideal time for scrying. In almost all weathers on a Monday night we wrap-up to sit-out in the yew grove near Martyr Worthy. We offer ale to one tree in particular, though it is enmeshed with the others; it commands the grove and shelters our rites. This offering also honours the local wights and ancestors; where roots writhe into earth and stone and bone (where the one ends and another begins seems an academic point to labour). We hammer-in, rattle bells, chant galdr, shake runes and press the meaning in the dark; heathens relating to our more-than-human worldscape.

Killing others with respect, eating them with impunity

Winter days are for another form of attempting respectful relationships: hunting. Where the condensation has cleared I can just make out Freyja sitting on her perch, settled on one leg, feathers puffed out in the freezing January cold; patiently, imperiously, looking out on her world, taking it all in as only a hawk's eyes can. I can walk out of my door, cross the road, wander a hundred yards down the lane, climb over a fence, and hunt with her along the riverbank up as far as Bere Mill, and down at Tufton too. I was worried she might have lead poisoning a couple of days ago: a piece of shot in her casting confirmed my fear that while I had lost her for a couple of hours she had killed a pheasant pricked by a shotgun. A succession of falconer's nightmares: a lost hawk, a poisoned hawk, a dead hawk – making the memory of a fine flight after a cock bird, which she caught that same day, and finding her after being lost; and that she is safe and well in her mews today, all the more valued and acute. She is now in her fourth hunting season. We have learned a lot since training started…

It is a bright, crisp day, December 2011. The journey through the lanes from home to our hunting ground took a quarter of an hour or so; not far. But we had come a long way to get to this point: the training had taken weeks, months, and all things considered we had both come on well. We now walked up the open hill a couple of hundred yards towards the treeline. Neither of us knew what lay ahead; joy, failure, injury and death had an equal chance. But I counselled myself, 'Wyrd goes as she should.' The partnership was about to be tested and I too was keen, felt the urgency, the crackle of excitement in the atmosphere. The hunt was on.

I cast her off, climb over the barbed wire and tread down the hostile brambles to make entry. I crouch to find a gap into the spinney, a naked birch switch scratches my cheek, my sleeve tears as I tug it free of the thorns. Life is strangled, persistent and vibrantly silent in this place; I feel sure my ungainly presence, unlike hers, is noticed. I beat the frost-wrought thicket with a blackthorn staff – cut on Mayday dawn from the woods near the cottage, seasoned over the summer months, waxed and polished by my own hand – the dead wood goading and chastening vigorous bushes to release their quarry. Then, quite distinctly, there's a rustle ahead – of fur or feather?

I shrink to my haunches, inadequately hiding a predatory frame and look keenly through a web of emerald-green algae-stained twigs. The cold yellow of early morning winter sunlight makes me squint. A flash of certainty, the split-second decision made, I cry out, 'Freyja,' and bark the time-honoured call: 'Ho! Ho! Ho!' The air is close, electric, a buzzing in my ears, quickening blood, vision too slow. It all happens in an instant. A flash of amber-black, she swoops past me, wings folded, primaries within a hair's-breadth of the oak branches, their bark torn and fissured by yawning age; her fanned tail twists left then right as she darts between the skin-like trunks of twilight-grey beech trees; over the wire and along the fence line one hundred yards or more; and then she's gone, out of sight. The ring of bells; a scream; deathly silence.

The moment before I run headlong after her, crashing through the bushes – a time between times, a heightened sense of place, of life and death, everything that has lived and died – a male blackbird stakes his claim in rich melody, the frost on the moss beneath my knee melts, a scarlet elf-cup toadstool looks suddenly so important and alive. Nature, this close up. I launch into the thicket following a narrow deer path, stooping under briar-rose thorns, dodging tussock-snares, narrowly losing my footing on a tooth-like nodule of flint protruding from the chalky soil, bared only now to daylight after lifetimes held deep within the earth.

I get there. She's got it. Holds it well. With a vice-like grip around the head, murderous talons piercing, feet crushing, ferocious killing – a rabbit's life-breath fallen. We both pant with the exertion of the chase, adrenaline pumping.

Need, like a stricture about the breast,
though oft a mortal sign, can augur well
when attended to quickly.

I intone runic letters, make the sign, give heart-felt life-firm thanks.

Year brings hope for men,
When Gods in haven permit the earth
to give forth bright crops for rich and poor.

Later, in the garden, I will pour a drink, an offering, at the thorn tree I planted. She begins to plume the fur and I help her feed-up on the neck, her reward, the rest my evening's supper.

Time returns and the landscape starts to speak coherently again. We are upon the Downs. The blackbird is silent now, but a pair of ravens croak languidly, knowingly, overhead; the lone cry of a scavenging buzzard, raptor-kin, follows. We are all interdependent. I feel a keen north-easterly pricking at my cheeks. A handsome piebald whinnies in the paddock. The Winterbourne shines in the valley below...

Hawking, walking and sitting with Gods and ancestors

Hunting with Freyja I am intimately connected with a wider-than-human world. I aim to kill with respect and eat others with impunity. I honour my Goddess. I follow in a long line of falconers, probably not from prehistory and certainly not unbroken, but there were falconers here from around the 5th century when heathen Germanic tribes migrated to England. I am not directly related to them, of course, but for me they are 'ancestors', broadly understood. My falconry connects me to the past and to the land and its persons in the present. I feel a connection, a stillness, a quickening, a deep sense of belonging elsewhere too; at the prehistoric monuments near where we hunt: Adam's Grave, Wayland's Smithy, Danebury, Stonehenge. I claim no more ownership over them than anyone else, but they are special to me, a part of my identity, as I have walked, been still, felt transformed, among them.

I spent a good time last summer on pilgrimage: including to Harewood Forest a few miles west of here, as well as to the cave art at Creswell Crags, the beeches and ramparts of Danebury hillfort, monuments in the Stonehenge landscape (now much more accessible and with a very good visitor centre, at last), the bluestones outcrops of the Preseli Hills, Coldrum long barrow and Sutton Hoo. In Harewood I found an ancient trackway with a long row of yew trees and growing from within one of these was an oak. I climbed onto one bough of the oak, sang galdr, cast runes and scryed. It became still, quiet, serene; things were clear.

I am Athelwynn.
I am wayfarer, out-sitter, seidrman.
Shut up! Listen: the wind whispers Woden;
Smell the rain on the ground carried by Thunor;
Taste the sea-salt-spray of Niordr and Ran;
Feel the land, the earth, Erce, our mother – where Mugwort
* grows, snakes slither and hawks do fly;*
And look out for the wights and ancestors dwelling in the trees,
* hills, dolmens and standing stones of this middle enclosure.*
We live in a more-than-human world. Celebrate.

Archaeologists, Pagans and ancestors

I have probably used up more than half of my life. I have identified as Pagan for nearly three of those decades. I have a loving partner who has been with me almost two decades. I have spent half that time gaining academic qualifications, and another decade or so working in academic life. I have been a falconer for four years. For now, that'll do and that's it. Half a life spent in four sentences.

I do not know whether there is an afterlife. I have not written a will or decided whether to be buried or cremated. I like the idea of my body returning to the earth, eaten up and made good use of by worms, bacteria and others (a fair and due return as I have had to eat others too), absorbed by the roots of plants, ultimately becoming earth; this regeneration making the ultimate connection to the land, to those living on it and within it, to ancestors; a quiet becoming of an ancestor, or part of the ancestral past, with little other impact on the world, just as it has been and will be for most people, human and 'other-than-human' (Harvey 2005).

Would I care if my remains endured and were excavated by archaeologists? I can't know. The dig would likely be accompanied by the due respect scientists give to their work, but it would be a particular kind of respect, somewhat analytical and remote. The excavation would be a disruption, a disconnection, destructive. Perhaps that's a fair trade for the knowledge that results. I don't know. I would just hope that at least one of those archaeologists was also Pagan, as of course some are. I can't gauge what sort of respect they might offer, but it would probably do. Making connection, relating, respecting others, is important for archaeologists, Pagans and ancestors.

A small minority of Pagans have called for the reburial of certain prehistoric human remains, which for them are important as Pagan 'ancestors' (Blain and Wallis 2007). This has brought them into contact and often contest with heritage managers and archaeologists, for whom the excavation and analysis of human remains is crucial to learning more about the past; is part of their job. This analysis can take many years due to the limited availability of funding for research, and the idea of reburying the remains is largely viewed as problematic, although there are examples of it, such as the recent case of the 2000BCE 'Queen of the Inch' from the Isle of Inchmarnock (BBC 2010). For archaeologists, reburial constrains future analysis, although not in all cases, as the re-excavation of cremated human remains from Stonehenge in 2008 shows. Other Pagans disagree with those calling for reburial, the group *Pagans for Archaeology* (archaeo-pagans.blogspot.com/) stating clearly the importance of archaeological work for revealing more about ancient Pagan religions, in turn informing today's Pagan practices (Ford 2009). The group *Honouring the Ancient Dead* (www.honour.org.uk), though not exclusively Pagan, seeks to work with all the interest groups in order to ensure prehistoric human remains are treated with respect, although what this might mean is an area of debate.

Aside from the issue of human remains, Pagans and archaeologists are usually allies. Archaeologists do not speak with one voice and Pagans certainly don't. There are archaeologists sympathetic to Pagans and there are various Pagans working in archaeology. Pagan archaeologists have an important role in all of this, as mediators. The stake-holders have to work together. It is important that they respect one another and one another's opinions, however contrary. It is important that they engage in consultation, collaborative dialogue, and informed decision-making (Wallis 2015); taking stepping stones to common ground (Swidler and Dongoske 1997).

Mouth is the shaper of speech,
Wisdom's prop and wise men's comfort,
and every peer's ease and hope.

Conclusion: Ancestors-wights-allies
Many people avoid labelling themselves for the good reason that terms simplify and obfuscate. 'Dr', 'Professor', 'heathen',

'falconer', and other titles, look strange together and surely refer to someone else? 'Gods', 'Goddesses', 'ancestors' and 'allies', might be discrete for others but for me they bleed into one another. We are never fixed and finished or all grown up, but are always becoming (Ingold 2006):

> *in the blood red robin red yew berry;*
> *on the chalk white bone white earth;*
> *from Grim's ditch to Grim's grave and the Wansdyke;*
> *where hawks, among other significant others, are companion species;*
>   (Haraway 2003)
> *when Mugwort, oldest of herbs, remembers and reveals;*
> *where Gods are ancestors, ancestors can be animals, some plants are*
>   *allies, and allies wights.*

Waes thu hael.

Bibliography

BBC News Glasgow and West Scotland 2010. *Queen of the Inch to be Re-interred* (18 August 2010). Online: http://www.bbc.co.uk/news/uk-scotland-glasgow-west-11010977 (accessed 31 August 2010).

Blain, Jenny and Wallis, Robert, J. 2007. *Sacred Sites, Contested Rites/Rights: Contemporary Pagan Engagements with Archaeological Monuments.* Sussex Academic Press, Brighton. Also: Wallis, Robert, J. 2003. *Shamans / neo-Shamans: Ecstasy, Alternative Archaeologies and Contemporary Pagans.* Routledge, London.

Ford, Nick 2009. *'Honouring the Ancient Dead': The Care of Elderly Souls and the Rights of Bone Fragments to a Quiet Life.* Online: http://pagantheologies.pbworks.com/w/page/13622300/The%20Care%20of%20Elderly%20Souls%20and%20the%20Rights%20of%20Bone%20Fragments%20to%20a%20Quiet%20Life (accessed January 13 2015).

Haraway, Donna 2003. *The Companion Species Manifesto: Dogs, People and Significant Otherness*. Chicago: Prickly Paradigm Press.

Harvey, Graham 2005. *Animism: Respecting the Living World*. London: Hurst & Company.

Ingold, Tim 2006. Rethinking the Animate, Re-Animating Thought. *Ethnos* 71(1): 9-20.

Johnson, N. J. and R. J. Wallis, 2015 [2005]. *Galdrbok: Practical Heathen Runecraft, Shamanism and Magic*. Second edition. The Wykeham Press, Winchester.

Swidler, Nina, E., Dongoske, K., Anyon R. and Downer Alan S. (eds.) 1997. *Native Americans and Archaeologists: Stepping Stones to Common Ground*. AltaMira Press, Walnut Creek, California.

Wallis, Robert, J. 2012. 'A Heathen in Place: Working with Mugwort as an Ally' in McLellan, G. and Cross, S. (eds.) *The Wanton Green: Contemporary Pagan Writings on Place*: 24-37. Mandrake, Oxford (translation by R.J.W). Also Wallis, Robert, J. 2010. 'In Mighty Revelation: The Nine Herbs Charm, Mugwort Lore and Elf-Persons – An Animic Approach to Anglo-Saxon Magick' in *Strange Attractor Journal* 4: 207-240.

Wallis, Robert, J. 2014. 'Re-examining Prehistoric Stone 'Wrist-guards' as Evidence for Falconry in Later Prehistoric Britain' in *Antiquity* 88(340): 411-424.

Wallis, Robert, J. (In press 2015). 'Pagans, Archaeology and Folklore in Twenty-first Century Britain: The Case of The Stonehenge Ancestors' in *Journal for the Academic Study of Religion: Special Issue: Religion, Archaeology and Folklore* 15(2).

Healing the Ancestral Communion: Pilgrimage Beyond Time and Space

By Caitlín Matthews

The guests are scatter'd thro' the land.
For the eye altering alters all.
(William Blake: *The Mental Traveller*)

Seeking the ancestors

Throughout life, we are in pilgrimage to the place of our true abiding. This longed-for place is a location that lies outside time, for it is really a condition whereby we are in communion with all that is and has been and will be: a totality of being that is within reach of all human beings, but that we somehow keep losing. It is intimately bound up with our ancestors, with whom we share the key to that condition.

I purposely use the terms 'pilgrimage' and 'communion' here as neutral words of useful meaning: for pilgrimage is just a sacred journey and communion is merely a state of being in union. But, oh, when you experience both of these for yourself, how quickly you can discard the 'just' and the 'merely' from your vocabulary! For when the pilgrimage leads you to the finding and the communion includes yourself within it, then your ancestors are indeed with you forever.

Who or what are the ancestors? In modernist culture, ancestry is usually understood in solely human terms, that ancestors are our human blood kindred from who we descend. But in traditional animist cultures throughout the world, from North America to Australia, ancestors are understood as *everything* that is, whether we would regard it as a sentient being, such as an animal or a tree, or as something we don't think of as alive, like a rock or the land we walk upon, or indeed, whether it would be regarded as having existence at all, such as a faery, a spirit, the presence of a deceased forebear, or a divinity. While such a view stretches our limited understanding, this traditional and comprehensive inclusion of everything as an ancestor also creates helpful pathways into exploring our ancestry and belonging.

I've spent a lifetime exploring just what ancestors are and where it is that we find them, an education triggered by the nature of the family into which I was born. Because my mother had been fostered on an aunt and uncle when she was only a few weeks old and grew up distant from her brothers and sisters and her mother and father, it meant that I also grew up without half my family. For my mother, this distance was a continuous sorrow that depressed and upset her as much at eight-five years of age as it had done when she was a child. For myself, this mysterious absence of physical forebears from my mother's side began to set my sights wider, to look beyond people for my ancestors. So I searched for clues everywhere, trying to understand and untangle my mother's sense of exile.

I remember when I was a child, how my father would drive our family out every weekend to the countryside, to different locations around the South Downs. Since we lived in an urban setting, these weekend visits were considered very important to our health as a family. As we travelled through these lovely places, I frequently experienced an inexpressible tenderness in which I and everything else was mysteriously participant in a wider embrace. I still experience these feelings whenever I am upon chalk downland: whether I see the bright bones of the exposed chalk downs or the ploughed up shards of chalk and flint that scatter the brown, marled furrows in autumn. I recognise this as my ancestral landscape.

As a child, the sense of the chalk filled my dreams. I would meditate upon these dreams, sitting snug in my den in the hollow of the chalk hillside, which is where I first discovered

Father Flint and Mother Chalk as spirit beings, the *genii loci* of the South Downs. These were the deep, primordial ancestors who spoke to my bones and marrow.

When later I researched my family genealogy, it came as no surprise to me to find that my paternal forebears had been farm labourers on the chalk back as far as records stretched into the late 16th century, living in one small village, until the industrialisation, enclosure and changes in agriculture drove them to the coast, where they became part of the naval machine then intent on defeating Napoleon at the end of the 18th century.

I mention this juncture in our history, the movement of people from the countryside to the town, because it marks a critical point when we began to lose our close contact with the nested realities that bring together the land, our ancestral belonging to it and our deeper understanding of our wider ancestry. Around this point, we became further exiled from our ancestors, who began to shift into more distant perspective. It is largely with the eyes of exiles that we now behold our ancestors. For us, they have become 'just human,' the mere end-result of family genealogy where we must be content with a list of names and dates, but no actual connection. Our task is to find the deeper ways of communion that are still available to us.

Primordial co-ordinates: our vertical and horizontal hold

It is the sorrow of all exiles that they cannot be upon their native soil anymore. When they relocate to another land, they will often speedily replicate all that made their land dear to them, so that its food, music, religion, culture and customs can help maintain that belonging. In some places, this movement can develop into a ghetto mentality whereby immigrants replicate their own culture to the extent that they have minimal assimilation into their new land. Exilic replication is an attempt to aid self-identity and reaffirm ancestral belonging in the face of despair and disorientation, but it often leaves the immigrant cut off from developing as a citizen of the new country. The children of immigrants usually assimilate more readily, since they have to learn the language and cultural values of the host country in order to fit in at school.

As a result of my own one-sided family, I was driven to explore what being Irish in Britain meant, since my mother's lost siblings were the children of Irish immigration. This led over many years of study to a deeper knowledge of Celtic culture and spiritual beliefs, about which I have extensively written and taught, and to the ancestral nature of my shamanic work in the community.

A great part of my teaching has been to visit the Celtic diaspora around the world, so I am familiar with the factor of replication. Whether I am asked to visit the United States or New Zealand, Australia or Nova Scotia, it is often to help resolve a significant sense of loss or disconnection that the children of immigrants are experiencing. Despite living half way round the world, or the fact that their ancestors departed Europe many generations ago, people still feel ancestrally Scottish, Irish or Welsh, even while being citizens of other countries. However, they are now living on a very different land mass that has its own culture and spiritual beliefs. They often feel cut off from ancestors, not only in spatial or territorial terms, but in temporal ways also. Their ancestry often feels to them as if it is in the past, rather than the present. What will make it more immediate?

Of course, it is impossible to replicate our human forebears' lives and conditions, even if such a thing were advisable. There are indeed many re-enactment groups who dress and speak as closely as they can to a desired historical era, and with painstaking research discover all that can be known and re-enacted. Ultimately, while this may satisfy on some level, such an action can become an exercise in fruitless replication, which further ghettoises that group and finally descends into escapist fantasy.

Those whose forebears fled persecution, war or economic hardship in order to try again elsewhere, laudably want to keep alive the ancestral culture from which they have sprung. Very many exiles do become successful settlers and still maintain a proud tradition in which language, art, music and custom figure large. Somewhere, sometime, there is a spiritual link to ancestors, they know, but it is a matter of how to rediscover it. Throughout the latter half of the 20th century, many children of immigrants have tried to overcome this sense of ancestral disconnection by attempting to make a bridgehead to the world's traditional cultures or to the ancestral wisdom of their host country, with mixed results.

A fairly typical response to this attempt was experienced by a student of mine in New Zealand who approached some Maori women she knew, asking if she might learn their ways. The Maori women retorted, 'Why, don't you have any traditions of your own?' Then, more kindly, they added, 'When you understand your own traditions, come back to us and we'll see.' My student set about doing just that, exploring her own cultural traditions from Britain and Europe, opening the long-closed door of Scottish wisdom for herself, so that she understood from whence she had come, which is how and why I came to be invited to New Zealand, just one of many visits I've made around the world to address this sense of ancestral disconnection. My work today has spread wider than just the Celtic diaspora, as other groups began to ask me to help them make reconnection with their ancestors.

When I've been asked to teach in countries that have been under recent dictatorship or suffered from oppressive or alien regimes, the task has usually been to first re-establish connection with the ancestors and traditions that precede those times – not with any agenda to replicate atavistic lore – but to re-establish a basic root connection. So, when I first taught in Portugal, I introduced my students to the ancient roots of Portugal, a primal task in a country where modernist culture has already overwhelmed even post-war folk understandings of the country, and where the influence of foreign and new age books translated into Portuguese outstripped those books that informed residents about their own cultural and spiritual traditions. In the Czech Republic, it was about rediscovering a primal energy and ancestral nourishment to help re-inspirit the hopes and minds of a people who declared their independence in 1987 and who redrew their country in 1993. The upheavals of two world wars, the displacement that they caused and the huge fracture between cultural ancestral continuity and the modern world also feature largely in the different parts of Europe where I teach.

This great privilege of enabling people to find and connect with their deeper ancestors has been wholly based upon finding the horizontal and vertical hold.

Let me explain: in the not-so-ancient days of my youth, analogue televisions came with what used to be called the horizontal and vertical hold. These were buttons that controlled how the picture was delivered to our tiny screens. Loss of horizontal synchronisation usually resulted in an unwatchable picture that looked like scribble; loss of vertical synchronisation would produce an image that rolled up or down the screen over and over. These two buttons enabled us to see the transmitted image as clearly as could be seen in that black-and-white era.

In our own time, a similar lack of primary co-ordinates in our spiritual lives is disabling understanding of and connection with our ancestors. Many receive a transmission that is like inter-ference or else are aware of a rolling picture that never becomes clear. We need both a horizontal and a vertical hold to help bring us into focus with our ancestors. These are needed not just by exiles and immigrants or those displaced by political and economic change, but by everyone who wants to access their ancestors and restore an essential communion.

Our 'horizontal hold' is what makes us a native of the place where we live, regardless of whether we were born there or not; it entails an intimate knowing of your place, and the shape of every season and direction; knowing and recognising the plants, rocks, animals and trees in your region; being aware of the spirits of that place, the unseen and manifest life both in, and out of time, in that location. When that relationship with the land is established, we begin to live in harmony with our place.

Our 'vertical hold' transects time and place, for it is made up of the ancestral, cultural and inspirational rivers that flow into our being. The ancestral tributaries are those of blood, of genetic and epigenetic tendency that inform and shape the life of our bodies, while the cultural and inspirational tributaries carry the influences that inform and shape our souls. When we begin to make connection with the ancestral currents that course through us, then ancestors of both blood and spirit become even more aware of us and we of them.

The result of a well-practised horizontal and vertical hold being in place is that we become established and seen: both in our communities where we can be of service, as well as to the unseen witnesses who observe and support us: the spirits and ancestors who are part of a living ancestral continuum.

With these primordial co-ordinates established, the real solution to lack of ancestral communion begins to be within reach. It lies in how we bring together the vertical hold of ancestry with the horizontal hold of the land on which we are living. By regarding our ancestors not merely as historical human forebears, but as our wider ancestry that goes beyond time and space, we enter into a more vital relationship with them, into the place of our true abiding where communion is restored.

The place of our true abiding

There is a timeless place outside time and space that always abides. It is medicine to the sick, and peace to the warrior, it is play to the child and knowledge to the scholar. But instead of being within it, we have abandoned it. The heartsick very much wish it existed, while the accepted social view is to deny any such time and place whatever.

The existence of life and its intelligence beyond time and space, within our own era, has become a matter for science rather than of metaphysics. An acceptance of the concept of spirits, disembodied presences or their mythic appearances is what now separates the believer from the non-believer. The gulf between rational and spiritual viewpoints has become a no-man's land, a flashpoint for mutual insult or mockery if anyone dares enter into it. Let us dare!

The place of our true abiding is a condition of being that is accessible when time is stilled, when space draws to a point. To enter into it, we need to make our bellies soft, to strip ourselves of the cladding with which we have become armoured, to step out of serial time and into timelessness. This brings us into a state of communion with all that is: a basic yet very sophisticated way in which everything is connected within an animist viewpoint. Since animism historically underlies all developed spiritualities, it is a helpful approach to us, since it comes without the baggage of religion.

The spiritual technologies whereby anyone can enter into the place of our true abiding range from ecstatic union via dance and song, through to quiet meditation. The purpose of entering into this state is to be in communion and connection with the deeper ancestors who see and know more of the universe than is possible from an individual perspective. From within that condition, we know with a wider consciousness, as in this poem that came from within that embrace, wherein I became aware of a Gaelic poet (unknown to me and himself aware of the ancestral communion in a time also unknown), who composed his work in the house of darkness, swimming like a salmon to the source of generation: the diminishing lines of each verse chart his progress from individual to ancestral consciousness which is a single and shared vision:

In Dazzling Darkness

Like the salmon now, he sleeps in the dim weed
Of metaphor, waiting for a sudden phosphorescence
To lead him to the bright, bestowing spring
Where he was born; to spawn from heart's need
A tale untold, uttered only in the dark,
Spun by every seeker of life's spark.

Only the young discover the narrow way through the rock;
The upstream struggle to be free brings them straight home
To the place of parenting; yet in the throes of generation
It means nothing but a sudden curvetting in foam,
A salmon's leap to reach the head of the loch.

In the house of darkness, the poet muses long
Into the night. To no luminary constant, spurning
Sun, moon and stars, to come to the place of turning,
Where he dances solitary, far from the chiding throng.

Tracing the threefold spirals of the entrancing dark,
He is purely given, in the way of his kind, to the gifting
Cauldron, the utter source and centre where he births and dies.

Behind his sightless, all-envisioning, lightless eyes,
The vision crests in the embrace of the primal parents,

And there is only darkness shattered by shards of eternity.

Within this condition of awareness, I could not tell whether he was myself or I him. The experience that we shared outside of time and space was received by me as an entwined knot of understanding, which only later meditation unfolded in serial time and temporal place as a poem. At the nexus of timelessness and spaciousness, everything comes together as a kernel of wisdom that is without price and beyond self.

As anyone who practices one of the spiritual technologies that enables entry into the place of our true abiding understands, this entering into communion is not a self-indulgent, self-centred nor a static practice, but rather an opportunity and meeting of kindred. It should not be necessary to say so, but such is the disconnection and fracture among us, that very many people are under the impression that any practice of spiritual technology must be entirely for the purposes of self-aggrandisement or individual satisfaction, because the recreational rather than the sacred is what modernist culture understands.

Let us be clear: we enter into communion with all that is sacred, whole and inviolable to be joined to it, to not be separate, and in that act we are made sacred, whole and inviolable in our whole being. Spiritual practice unites what is fractured and separate, which is why practitioners repeat their practice daily. When spiritual practice is avoided for lengthy periods, then the practitioner becomes disconnected.

What happens within this state of communion and how do we express or reflect it? The common language throughout world cultures is metaphor: poetry, dream, song, vision, prayer and story are the language of our meeting. In such a way we may experience distinct scenes wherein a collective of ancestors of different times and places are present, or a sense of specific spiritual allies who come close. There may be dialogue that is unspoken, but nonetheless understood, or a silent communion of meaning and wonder. Sometimes the communion is experienced sensationally in the cells of the body rather than as visual scenes. Knowing and recognising from a wider source of intelligence are part of the communion.

But to speak of these things out of context is not helpful without some personal experience. Our true teachers are the earth, our ancestors and kindred, and we cannot proceed until we are prepared to open our awareness to them. To clarify the concepts and technologies I am talking about here, I will address how we approach gaining control over our horizontal and vertical holds, so that the place of your true abiding becomes clear.

The place where you stand now

There are three kinds of places that can be helpful in establishing your horizontal hold: the place where you are right now, the places that call to you powerfully, and the place of your birth. Let us explore the possibilities.

The place where you are right now is perfectly suited to begin your practice. Just as ancestors are not only human, but inclusive of everything between heaven and earth now, then and when, so too all places on the earth share a living connection. Wherever we stand upon the earth, we are simultaneously able to be mindful of it all from that one place.

This basic practice, *Form for Establishing Relationships,* is one that you can use in any place. Whether you are inside or outside, stand and fuse your awareness with your body, using all your senses to experience what is to be present in that place. With soft belly and easy breath, regard what it is like to be present there, without expectation or agenda (Matthews Forthcoming).

1. Sink your awareness down into the heart of the earth: what do you experience? What relationship do you have with the deep below?
2. Send your awareness up into the sky: what relationship do you have with it? What is the relationship of the sky with the earth, and the earth with the sky? What do you receive in that relationship?
3. Now regard the direction ahead of you with all your senses: what do you notice? What is the relationship

between you and the way ahead?

4. Repeat 3 with the direction behind, and to your left and right, with all your senses.

5. Now repeat 1-4 with your eyes closed. What lies behind what your senses tell you of the six directions? Keep your belly soft and your breath easy. Be aware of what arises in your understanding.

6. Thank the place where you have been standing and acknowledge your kinship with it.

7. Now consider what has changed. What is your relationship with the place where you stand?

As you did this, you may have been aware of things outside of you: noises, sights, feelings and sensations received by your senses. If you were outside, you have been aware of people, animals, clouds that came into your line of sight. How did that feed into your findings? What did you learn when you closed your eyes? What metaphors, understandings, stories or scenes were you aware of? How did the six directions show themselves to you?

The deeper levels of awareness that occur when you close your eyes will have revealed to you something else about the six directions. By regarding a place from the standpoint of both your inner awareness and your outer senses, you sew together the two sides of reality that make up that place: you become aware of not only the physical life and appearance that surrounds that place, but also the invisible – yet just as real – life and appearance that is also present all the time. This realisation usually lies beneath the level of ordinary awareness and is easily blocked or denied as 'irrelevant' or 'mere fantasy'. However, by bringing your realisations up from the deep well of awareness, you change the relationship you have with the earth. As you repeat this practice – which is a daily, regular communion with the place where you live – your questions and understanding will also change. You soon realise that a place is not discreet nor separate from what lives on it: you and the place are there with many others, and the interpenetration of one side of reality with the other is a constant interplay and dialogue in which you are participant.

The earth as ancestor

Of course, the earth is also our ancestor. It physically nourishes us as a mother and supports our life as a father. Just as our DNA and our physical characteristics bear the clear traces of our human blood kindred so too our body-field holds the signature of our place of birth. I have learned over the years that the common denominator of help and healing lies with the spirit of the land, on which I unashamedly draw in my shamanic work. Most of my healing practice is concerned with restoring connection with ancestors, and with healing fragmentation or loss caused by trauma, family disorientation or vocational dislocation.

To understand what is happening within a client's being, I work by a form of echo-location or ultrasound, whereby I send sound into the client's body in order to assess what is held in the body-field. Closing my eyes and feeling through my outstretched hand I pick up what is present through a mixture of sound and feeling. Held within the body-field are a nesting set of realities, the most immediate of which is the imprint of the land where someone was born or the landscape in which they grew up. For example, the landscape imprint of someone who was born in Africa, even if they lived there for a very brief time, is unmistakable: this landscape has an overwhelming signature that sings out. The imprint of other places may not be as strong as this, but as I sing into the body-field, I receive impression of hills, rivers, plants, animals and so on. As these impressions arise, so I sing them aloud that the client might also hear and remember this profound level of their being. Whatever else is held or entangled with their being, this primary landscape level helps restore conscious connection with the land as ancestor. The song that is arising enables their remembrance.

Clients will often weep in recognition of these landscapes, once so familiar to them, even though those places may now be changed beyond recognition because of building, alteration or flood, yet they remain ancestral places that give life and healing. For myself, I am acutely aware of the client as *being the landscape* in which fish swim, on whose shoulders flowers grow, whose limbs are the groins of mountains and rivers. I behold each person as one with the primal landscape that has shaped and nourished their body, and I sing the songs that arise spontaneously from the groins of the land.

This is why working with the place of our birth can be of great help, even if you now living distant from it, for it can reset the default of our 'factory settings' – those encodings in our cells that we received by being born in a particular place. Unfortunately, for many people, the place of their birth is inextricably entangled with their parental home, which may not be a pleasant memory because they were not properly welcomed there or even introduced to that location in a good way. For anyone with that problem, it is important to be reconciled with the place of birth, by understanding the place as a wiser ancestor than the parents or immediate forebears who raised you, so that you are not continually in reaction from the earth itself.

By using the *Establishing Relationship* form above, you too can restore your relationship with the place of your birth. You do not need to be physically present because your awareness can travel where it needs to – remember, every place on the earth is connected. Even if the place of your birth is altered beyond recognition or no longer present due to environmental changes or urbanisation, in your awareness it remains outside of time.

Sit in a quiet place and connect the place where you are with the place of your birth. Remember that you are primarily visiting the place on the earth where you were born, not the home of your birth family, if this is problematic to you. You are going to be there, as for the first time.

1. As you sit quietly with closed eyes, the birth-place is now under your feet. Using the basic form of *Establishing Relationship* form in the pages above as your practice, explore your relationship with the six directions as a person newly born at this location.

2. Be aware of the welcome that you receive from the place and take that into your body. If difficult or unhelpful remembrances come to your mind, return again to the soft belly and the easy breathing of a newborn: allow that first breath of life to come to you again and, with the spacious awareness of a newborn, be aware of the directions in turn.

3. When you have experienced all six directions, return to your centre, the hidden seventh direction of 'within' where you quietly absorb without any striving for remembrance all that happened to you. Allow the cells of your body to receive the experience and trust them to keep it safe.

4. When you have absorbed the experience of your birth place, return in awareness to the place where you are physically sitting.

5. Thank the place where you were born and acknowledge your kinship with it.

How does your relationship with the birth-place change? Of what are you now aware? Be aware of your body and how it feels: it isn't the body of newborn, but the body of adult now, yet something will be new. Be aware of the life within you as strengthened.

Just as there are imprints of the land and place of our birth within our body-field, so too there are ancestral imprints in the land itself that speak to us strongly. We instinctively know when certain places have a special depth, an indefinable call that goes straight to the viscera. These are places that want to be visited and which will call us back to them again until we know the spirit of the place better. We call them sacred sites or power places. As my dear friend, Jo May, who was the custodian of such a site for many years, wisely wrote: 'Ancient power spots and sacred sites...are gateways. The real openings lie in our own hearts, minds, and lives.' (May 1996)

Whether the place that calls to you is a landscape feature – a hill, wood, spring or river – or a place where ancestors have left remains of their circles, temples or holy places, these are powerful threshold points at whose nexus the energies of both sides of reality flow together and create a foyer or meeting place where time and place melt. A threshold is a place of crossing over, a boundary and border between two states: outside and inside, here and there.

You can use the *Establishing Relationship* form at or near sacred places also, learning what lies beyond these thresholds and how you pass through them.

Approach such thresholds respectfully, ensuring that the place is awake and welcoming. If you do not sense this welcome, find a place that is awake and willing to be in relationship with you. Some sacred sites are decommissioned, shut down or not currently operative, and to attempt speaking with them is like trying to address a sleeping person. If the place is very populous with visitors, either withdraw to a quieter place nearby or journey back to the threshold in meditation as you have done above with the place of your birth.

As you return to the one of the three kinds of place through the *Establishing Relationship* form, whether it is where you live now, the place of your birth or one of the sacred thresholds, you will begin to meet certain allies that naturally arise from these meeting places. These can be in many forms of kindred: plant, animal, faery or human ancestors. Greet them courteously. Learn what kind of relationship is between you. Those who return again and again to greet you become trusted allies who act as companions on your pilgrimage.

These sacred places powerfully restore and regenerate us, giving us opportunity to enter into the ancestral communion with spirits of land; the faeries, animals and plants who live in the wild places and the human ancestors who are accessible at the ancient sacred sites. When we visit a place, its inhabitants also see us. A very ancient method of initiation in these islands involves forming a deep relationship with such a threshold place over a long period of time, becoming purposefully attuned to it. In this way, all the kindred attuned to that place are like pitched orchestral instruments tuned together into a single harmony.

When we are in a good relationship with our place on earth, we learn how to cultivate a generous heart, for the gifts of the earth are expansive. Maintaining our relationship with our place on earth is a sacred trust that we must continuously uphold: the horizontal hold that keeps us firmly grounded. To maintain the vertical hold of ancestry, we need to recognise our kindred.

Recognising kindred

If we hold the animist viewpoint of the inclusive ancestors, not just human ancestors, then it also follows that everything is kin to us. This radically changes the relationship we have with the world. The sea gull flying past my window is kin, the fire burning in the brazier is kin, the tree in the garden and the yarrow growing by the path are my cousins. All that has been, is and will be is kin to me. In traditional societies this understanding is often recognised in a very immediate way where older humans are regarded as 'grandfather and grandmother' and addressed as such, while people of the same age as yourself are called 'brother and sister' and younger people 'son or daughter' or 'nephew and niece'. Perhaps the nearest we last came to this form of address was in the Elizabethan era when loosely-related people called each other 'coz' or cousin.[1]

In traditional societies the nature of non-human ancestors and kindred is noted in a similar way. Some ancestors are seen as wise elders who have a longer view, for they have endured longest: the earth itself, the wind, fire, rivers, and seas. Other ancestors and kindred have specific intelligence and wisdom, acting as guides and mentors to life, like a circle of elders: they are specific animals, plants, trees, wise humans whose deeds benefit many. These ancestors form a collective of wisdom to which we can always apply. Some are younger and less experienced, or innocent and unknowing: humans and the recently deceased ones who are still learning to be ancestors.

It is interesting to note that many of the culture heroes who bring civilisation, fire and technology to the earth in many folk stories and myths worldwide take the form of animals in whom we easily recognise elements of our human selves in trickery, cunning or intelligence: Coyote, Raven, Hare, Spider (Matthews 2010).

With our non-human kindred there comes respect. If the land is kin to us, being senior, then it deserves a special respect. If my actions towards the land divert or pollute a river, the consequences are severe, not just to the waters themselves, but to all my kindred who live and depend on the gifts of those waters, including those unborn of many species. Considering the consequences upon kindred to the ninth generation yet to come is normal to traditional societies. This is in stark contrast to the disregard of any consequences upon even our children that are so often part of short-term government decisions and considered normal within modernist society.

The shape of inclusive ancestry is as a circle of life, whereas the human ancestry model is seen as an evolutionary pyramid. It is a humbling and even-handed thing to accept yourself as but one being in the circle of life. But unless you see yourself as part of the circle, then you cannot understand how you affect the whole circle of life. If your mindset elevates you above land, animals and plants, then you will despise them or reckon them to be of no account. If you see the gifts of the land as only of commercial potential, then exploitation will result. We can readily see to what ends our ignoring wider and inclusive ancestry has already brought us.

The pan-Celtic peoples of Europe used to swear by the three most enduring things in order to demonstrate their determination to uphold their sacred word in an agreement. It went like this: 'May I keep faith with you or may the sky fall upon me and crush me, may the earth open and swallow me, may the seas rush in and drown me.' (Matthews 1989) In our own era, we have the ability to make all these three things happen, to pollute and alter the air, the earth and the waters. The terrain of our descendents will be different from our own. The things on which we depend have been altered unutterably, from the atmosphere that we breathe to the chemicals that are now within our bodies.

By ignoring the land and all that is upon it as an ancestor, we are also ignoring our own body and our kindred. Jeannette Armstrong, an indigenous Okanagan-Canadian writer, tells us that in the Okanagan language the word for 'body' also contains the word for 'land'. She writes, 'Every time I say that word... I realise that I am from the land...and that my body is the land.' (Nelson 2008) Among her people, it is believed that the land feeds them, but also that the people feed the land, by laying their bodies within it when they die. There is a true reciprocation in the love and care between people and their land.

You can try this for yourself: create some sentences in which the words for land/body have the same value: 'My body/land is weary,' or 'My land/body needs cultivation.' Feel what that understanding does in the cells of your body, how it expands the clasp of your mind. Fostering this mindset is essential for us now because we must establish the most simple and essential bonds that heal and nourish our ancestral communion, not only for ourselves and for the ancestors who stand behind us, but also for those yet to be born. In his poem, *The Mental Traveller*, where the cause and effect of life's unconscious decisions are horribly revealed, William Blake starkly tells us:

> *The guests are scatter'd thro' the land.*
> *For the eye altering alters all*
>   (Keynes 1975)

The guests – our kindred of many natures – have indeed been scattered by the way that our viewpoint has changed, but when we return to good relationship with our kindred, we learn how to cultivate a loving heart, for the gift of ancestors includes us, helping ourselves and others to come home, to see things differently and view the original contract we had with life.

The communion that is between ourselves, our kindred and our earth remains the single most binding ancestral commitment we will ever have. Each of us is responsible for its upkeep, though no-one imposes us it upon us. The ancestral communion is not bound by time; it is an eternal and continuous pilgrimage that we make to it.

Restoring the ancestral communion

Currently, many people hold themselves outside the ancestral communion: they do not even think of ancestors as an ongoing collective with whom we can have communion. For many, human ancestors are seen as just the recently dead of the past few generations, people with whom they are entangled or conflicted, or who are not likely to be helpful or supportive. But further back down the generations, human ancestors are of a different order, of course, where they are part of the wider collective. When human ancestors are seen to be problematic, an elegant solution is to go wider and seek out the non-human kindred and ancestry who *can* support us, for not all ancestors are in the same condition.

Our ancestors can be understood as partaking in one of the three major conditions:

1. *The recent ancestors* who are immediate forebears, known to us through living memory. These are apprentice ancestors, if you like, not yet fully immersed into the ancestral state.
2. *The historic forebears,* not personally known to us, but further back in time, including both our collateral human lineage as well as ancestors of other kinds. These include specific, wise ancestors who can mentor us from their particular skills, secure in the ancestral wisdom that supports them.
3. *The collective ancestors* from whom we all descend, who are in a variety of different kinds and species. These ancestors have group consciousness as part of one being, having become immersed entirely into the ancestral condition. Their wisdom is the most secure and wide-ranging.

The form for *Initiating Ancestral Communion* below can be used for contacting any of these different conditions of ancestors, but you will probably find most help from those ancestors and allies who have arisen from the *Establishing Relationship* form and already shown themselves to you: start with them.

1. Using the place where you are now or a sacred threshold as your starting point, establish relationship with the six directions.
2. Call upon one of the trusted allies who have arisen from using the *Establishing Relationship* form to help you now: your intention is to initiate ancestral communion.
3. Allow the ally to be your companion. Keep your breathing easy and your belly soft, as together you enter into the seventh direction, which lies at the heart of the six directions. This is a state that is neither within nor without, but

beyond time and space. It includes all that is.

4. Without striving, be a welcome visitor within that communion that is always happening. You do not have to ask questions, or discursively discuss with your ally what is happening. Just be included.

5. As time slows and place dissolves, be within the welcome.

6. You may be aware of other kindred here with you, of many different kinds: they are as welcome as yourself. One or more of them may be revealed to you.

7. Allow the cells of your body to remember what is experienced here. When time begins to flow again, return from within the communion to the place where you started.

Ancestral communion is an ongoing dialogue in which our whole being is in communication with the wider life of our planet. However long you have lived, no matter how intelligent you believe yourself to be, the wider ancestors are still older and share a collective wisdom to which no one person can aspire. This is why we need to listen and act upon our listening within that communion. The threshold places and times where the soul makes meeting become important – whether it is at a sacred site or a tree, whether it is at twilight or dawn when you hear most clearly. Here you can step out of place and time and make the pilgrimage to your ancestors. Greet them and thank them every day.

After you have initiated the ancestral communion, whether the issues that concern you be personal or collective, you can take them to the ancestors within the place of your true abiding for help, healing or understanding. This may be received within the ancestral communion itself, within your dreams or in everyday life when the realisation of its reality strikes you.

In some Eastern forms of meditation, the spaces between the practice are held as being as important as the practice itself: it is so with the ancestral communion. Even when you are not within it, it remains a reality to you. While you may not remain within it consciously for a long period of time, yet it is a condition that you understand and enter into when a larger focus is necessary, when being just human is too constraining. After you become familiar with the two forms given above, you will grow fluent enough to be able to pass momentarily into it wherever you are. The everyday life that you live, when lived with awareness of the ancestral communion and what it implies, becomes infused with your practice.

You find that you can inspire your near kindred so that the farthest kindred may be blessed in times yet to be, for you are contributory to the ancestral communion, not just a recipient of it. Every day you remember the kindred who are with you and are supported and witnessed by them. In your decisions, you consider those descendants yet to come, as well as asking help of those who've been, so that you choose responsibility.

By entering into the place of our true abiding, we cancel the constraints of time and space, we come home to ourselves and so we become accessible to all of our ancestors. We are part of a continuity of life that has been going on and will be going on and every exile we experience is yet another opportunity to come home.

On any pilgrimage, as the author Ian Sinclair has noticed: 'Who you walk with, alters what you see.' (Sinclair 2005) Those kindred who walk with us, from whichever of the ancestral conditions, help us understand differently. The recent forebears may have questions, dislikes and reactions; the historic forebears may point out distinct features in the landscape of our walk that keep us strong; the collective ancestors may enable us to be part of the pilgrimage in ways that transcend and also include the senses. Each shows us hand-holds and footpaths, though it is our own hands and feet that are walking the pilgrim way now. Ancestral communion isn't a fantasy, but a possibility from which springs our very future. You can help shape it well, my brothers and sisters, by your pilgrimage.

The place of our true abiding turns out to be our sense of family, the way in which we are kindred to all that is, throughout time and beyond space. In that timeless communion, with the ancestors behind us, round and ahead of us we can finally come home.

Bibliography

Keynes, Geoffrey (ed.) 1975. *Poetry and Prose of William Blake*. Nonesuch Library, Soho, London.

Matthews, Caitlín 1989. *The Elements of the Celtic Tradition*. Element Books, Shaftesbury.

Matthews, John & Caitlín 2010. *The Encyclopedia of Magical Creatures*, Harper Collins, London.

Matthews, Caitlín. Forthcoming. *The Book of Ancestral Welcome: Re-Membering the Wisdom of Our Ancestors*. www.hallow quest.org.uk

May, Jo, F. 1996. *Gateway Into the Underworld*. Gothic Image Publications, Glastonbury.

Nelson, Melissa, K. (ed.) 2008. *Original Instructions: Indigenous Teachings for a Sustainable Future*. Bear & Co. Rochester, Vermont.

Sinclair, Ian 2005. *Edge of the Orison: In the Traces of John Clare's Journey Out of Essex*. Penguin, London.

Memory at Sites of Non-Place: A Eulogy

By Camelia Elias

If I were asked which of all the mysteries will remain forever impenetrable, I would not hesitate to answer: the obvious.
(Edmond Jabès, 1989)

'By Imbolc,' the editor of this anthology requested that all the contributors here should address *This Ancient Heart*; a deadline of the time when all things should rise up again. A challenge, obviously. A thought I could not explain urged me on to say out loud: 'Symmetry. It's all about symmetry. The Ancient Heart knows symmetry and tradition that goes beyond time.' I was trying to get a sense of this idea in the context of what I had announced I'd be writing about in this piece; namely, two aspects of the way in which we can rethink engaging with our ancestral heritage: memory and its relation to the here and now.

As all our memories are based on describing the experience of a moment, they are prone to value judgments. As we often say: 'In hindsight, I think that *this* is what *actually* happened.' Also, in the context of ancestral history, the question that we all want to answer is: 'Whose memories am I now talking about?' But this essay is not a contemplation on what we know of memory, nor its function in historical research. This essay is about how we can create a memory of places and people we have never met as we let ourselves stumble on what we conveniently can assume are the workings of the heart. Even Shakespeare used to say that if you don't know what to do, or even what you're talking about, go knock on your heart, and it will tell you.[1]

I have in front of me a special issue of *The New Celtic Review* created by the Chief Druid of the Golden Section Order Society, Colin Murray, Issue 35, 'Brigantia' (February-April 1984).[2]

Throughout the 1970s and 80s Murray was responsible for the revival of all things Celtic in a way that was quite unprecedented. His journal was made with the illuminated manuscripts of medieval time in mind. All the covers were hand painted, and the interior featured handwriting along with the most amazing photographs that Murray himself took of ancient sites.

A look through this material discloses immediately a love of symmetry that goes beyond reason. Murray was an architect and he had a sense for the straight line. At the same time, the circle informs all of his thinking. He died at the age of 44 from ingesting yew tree leaves. From the standpoint of storytelling, Murray's life and death strike me as fascinating, precisely as it ties in with the man's sense of symmetry and what he was trying to achieve, almost from a place that can be identified as developing a method of loci, or the art of memory that tried to repossess old knowledge via visual and oral modes of transmission.

Murray was a man who had made a pact with trees. He said this much himself on a number of occasions, when he also recounted that his 'interest' in trees came as a result of a motorcycle accident in the 1970s, when he almost died[3]. In other words, for him, trees had become mediators between life and death. I find attractive the idea that some notions reach us at a particular time, neither too late nor too early, and that somehow it has to do with what we make of the calling of the heart. What we call the Ancient Heart has to do with the ineffability of the mystery that always stares us in the face. But how do we know it? When the Ancient Heart speaks, it tells us that the answer is not only in the past, but also in the way in which we consciously allow the past to become part of us, right here and now.

My contemplative mode here and desire to issue pronouncements have extended to discussing this thought with a chemist friend, and fellow spiritual walker of the web of life, Miguel Marques. He made the following remark:

Symmetry *becomes it.* I remember reading Emily Brontë's work and getting this feeling she felt that she belonged on the moors, not with civilisation; that her world was primal and natural and lawless. She was like a spirit in the wind, only to be shackled by norms and society. There's a wonderful thought from her sister, Charlotte, that Emily needed an interpreter to be able to function in this world. Perhaps Colin Murray felt more or less the same way. (Private correspondence)

Looking through his work it is clear that Murray wanted to restore the historical symmetry of the culture of the people whom he thought were breathing through correspondences, and the belief that, indeed, 'as above so is below'.

In his editorial introduction to Brigantia, he states the following:

This issue of *The New Celtic Review* is at last beginning to demonstrate the extraordinary range and scope of Pan Celtic Culture. What is abundantly clear, is that if we have 2,500 years of culture behind us, then there must be an equal amount of future History that has yet to be created [...] The pen is mightier than the sword – let us scorn our enemies with faint praise and turn our energies to the creation of the next 2,500 years of Pan Celtic Heritage. (Murray, 1984: 1)

Two years after these words, Murray died. What happened to walking the straight line, and to advocating for restoring symmetrical relations between cultures and historical peoples? What happened to the Ancient Heart?

Murray's introductory words here mirror his words in his own contribution to Brigantia, 'The Golden Section: The Pentagram', dealing with the concern and wisdom of knowing one's place. He begins this essay with the following remark: 'The

Rev William Borlace, writing in the mid 18th century upon his master work 'Observations upon the Antiquities of Cornwall' observed that 'The Druids always walked upon Pentagrams...'' (1758: 22).

What is fascinating here is the idea that one can technically walk on symmetry, and that by doing so, one remembers to embody the old saying: 'Home is where the heart is'. But locating where the heart resides is one of the tallest orders, with many mystery traditions placing it ultimately within the space of what can be termed a non-place.

Perhaps one of the greatest disappointments that most contemporary spiritual communities experience is the realisation that there's no symmetrical relation between the idealism of keeping all things in balance and the rhythm of the breathing world inside a non-place, the place whence one is ready to give more than others are ready to receive. As far as I am concerned, such publications as *The New Celtic Review* are often pervaded by the spirit of a single person in search of the Golden Fleece, 'the thing itself', or Section, as is the case here. There is very little that can explain the rigor, complexity, life-force and enthusiasm that go into such works. I find that what people such as Colin Murray tried to do is give readers a sense of what it means to create a repository of memory.

Almost each illustration in the journal can be said to activate the memory function in such a way that allows us to make visual correspondences to precepts of knowledge and wisdom across different cultural times and perceptions. To the journal are appended large illuminated posters, coloured in hand and topped with real gold and silver, each featuring a specific topic, such as a stone circle, the legend of the zodiac on the earth, or the Celtic pentagrams.

Through storytelling and through narrating the points of departure we can transmit to the next generation what we have in mind, or rather, what we have in our heart. By allowing correspondences to manifest, we create a history that goes beyond history. For instance, we can use our body parts as point of departure for the telling of the story of creation or our place in the larger universe. A story written on the basis of creating awareness around the symmetrical and symbiotic relation between, say, our head and a ram sitting on it and poking our temples and nerves with its horns, makes us forget about hierarchy. Walking on fish while carrying a crayfish inside our bosom makes us think that there's power we can draw on which has little to do with anthropocentrism.

There is symmetry between us and the creatures we share this planet with.

When I was asked by the editor of this anthology to offer a 'secular solution' to the problem of the self in an ancestral context, I first wanted to know what the problem really is, and where we can locate it. But then I realised that the whole point with such an anthology that calls to our awareness of how we might rethink the self along the path of the Ancient Heart is that the problem is everywhere, and that it is located perhaps in forgetfulness and disconnectedness. Secular solutions to how we tackle the problem of having forgotten the 'old ways' – if one may be presumptuous enough to suggest that the old ways were good ways, when we have little historical evidence for it, given also that history repeats itself – is to devise all sorts of commemorative events that celebrate with a plaque or a stone, or a reconstruction of sacred sites, what we imagine was 'better'. But better in what sense, and is 'spiritual tourism' and making pilgrimages to these sacred sites enough to restore in ourselves what we have forgotten? And what have we forgotten exactly?

Rather than come up with yet another set of solutions to the problem, perhaps the reason why I wanted to start this essay with making a reference to exceptional work and people thinking extraordinary thoughts is because I want to suggest that if we have a problem, then it's one of breathing. We have forgotten to breathe with nature, its fires, waters, and telluric forces. We have forgotten to listen to nature's own breathing, its breeze into our hair, and kiss on our skin. Publications such as Murray's that insist on hand tracings that may transport us to a time when we wrote with the body, bent over the smell of the earth and its ink, tell us that what the world struggles with is self-deluding emotions. Where is the body in our lamentations? Where is the colour? I wonder what Murray saw in the yew tree leaves. What message did he get on his last trip? The legacy he left us is the kind of interstitial non-place intended to remind us of the logic of one-to-one, perfect mappings. The rainbow of colours on the covers of his journals, the large posters done on architect paper, depicting stone circles captured in a poetic time and space and measured according to the science of the senses puts us on a track to considering what else is there beyond binary structures. And are they symmetrical too? And if they are not, what then? What memories are hiding there in plain sight? Any repository of memory will have this primary function: to remind us of how to allow first for a problem to become part of ourselves before we then can offer a solution.

Although I'm not always convinced that everything can be addressed from the standpoint of a structuralist approach focusing on binary relations, such as male/female, pretty/ugly, light/shadow, etc., which many neo-Pagan traditions return to and operate with, the fact that we can allow for something that evades these categories to become part of ourselves makes me value the importance of the remains. Imbolc is around the corner, but I want to talk about ashes. I want to say something about the necessity to die in one story to be reborn in another that has the Ancient Heart in the right place. What I find profound in this idea is the fact that the structuralism of opposites relies very much on its own undoing. For instance, the part that is always larger, or more 'ancient', the asymmetrical poetic line that ends a life of symmetry at odds with itself, or the thing that is not equivalent to the anticipated, but that rather escapes it, has the potential to disrupt the neat symmetrical dichotomies. What has the death of this Druid Chief left on the project of restoring 2,500 years of lost spirit and culture?

Any wound presupposes a pain that is unique, and that is impossible to get a sense of when it is not your own. I find that in this wounding all hierarchies dissolve. The larger thing, or the scattered ashes that mark our transformation, is not 'better' or 'higher', or better because it's active as against passive, or higher because it's bursting with energy as against receptive, but rather an encompassing tracing of all that is. I find that it is this very trace(ing) that has value, as it unsettles all we want to decide 'is so'. Colin Murray was a master at tracing, and it looks like his work is reborn in these very words. Could this be the Ancient Heart opening new doors to sacred space, to yet another stone circle made of ink and an oracular voice that wakes it?

In a manner of speaking all ancient ritual places have become a non-place. People go there because they want a sense of history, not because they have evidence of culture and civilisation. Some would ask, isn't that the same thing? And I would answer, 'No, it isn't.' What we call history is based on evidence of artifacts, not evidence of time before time, the time when we would roam on the earth free and in symmetry and communion with other creatures. Historians give us a sense of place based on circumstantial evidence: 'Here is a pot, here a piece of jewellery. This body was tattooed and mummified presumably because of sacrificial reasons. The people who lived here were probably like this... Come ye, to this brand new museum, which we have decided to call – until someone will contest the name, and make other claims – come ye, and learn about your ancestors.'

Without assuming a merely judgmental position here, I want to make the obvious observation that this kind of historical discovery and discourse produces tourism, not a real sense of how we can acquire a genuine appreciation of the ground we stand on. If I should attempt to define what the Ancient Heart is, I would say that it is the heart that goes before time, before the time of history and evidence, before the time when we started measuring, quantifying and qualifying according to states of cultural pre-condition.

As a teacher – both within and outside of the university – I often come across students who want to learn about what it means to be spiritual. Some of these students are looking precisely for a secular solution to the problem of forgetting and disconnectedness, one which bypasses the mainstream idea of making everything visible. Nowadays academics must make their discourse not only visible, but also relevant. The same applies to most spiritual leaders. You can't sell an idea, if you won't make it accessible to a field of visibility. Often this translates into verbal and written communication disseminated through all the social media. According to this protocol of visibility, the Ancient Heart must be articulated into words, put on paper for posterity, and then moved out into a museum.

Modern returns to pre-modern forms of narratives about the 'thing itself', 'truth and beauty', or the 'symmetry of the sacred' often manifest on the plane of the visible and the tangible. But the Ancient Heart has eluded that grasp. Poets would call the Ancient Heart ambiguity itself. Without ambiguity everything would end in a mediocre rut. In this sense, the Ancient Heart has always occupied the space of the 'non-place', where what is felt most strongly on the invisible level are first all the telluric forces, the stellar power, and then the breathing of the winds and waters in between heavens. A non-place defined along these terms gives us a sense of history before the time of history. The Ancient Heart must be an expression of that, of the time before time, and of symmetry that can afford to go astray. Before we can identify what has been forgotten, so that we can find a solution for it, we must try to remember how nature hit us in the gut outside of pacts and systems of correspondences.

In our secular attempts to return to the power of the Ancient Heart, we often try to invent taxonomies in response to the problem of forgetting what and how we feel outside of what we think we ought to feel. But these attempts create hierarchies based on the assumption that ancient civilisations were devoid of struggles for power. There is a tendency in new interdisciplinary anthropological studies of ancient cultures to combine classical scholarship with 'getting involved', yet the latter comes at the expense of losing sight of common sense, unless that partici-pation is experienced and reflected upon subjectively.

Recently I have come across the popular work of Martha Beck, a Harvard-educated sociologist, life-coach, and bestseller author, who has presented some of these taxonomies in her book, *Finding Your Way in a Wild New World* (2012). As most books of this type go, the idea is to present the reader with truncated visions of how we can reach a state of enlightenment. Beck's argument is that we function best when we can find a way to apply reason and magic to our lives in equal measure. We must learn the four steps, she claims, the steps that our ancestors were taking in their daily lives, and learn the ways of, 'Wordlessness, Oneness, Imagination, and Forming.' While I can see the point, I resist the reductionist type of narrative that describes 'steps' towards getting in touch with what is identified as a need to redefine our Ancient Heart. Perhaps last year it was seven steps. Now we are down to four.

Beck's primary claim is that the people of the ancient cultures were all magical people because they all knew how to work with applied reason and magic in context. They were all shamans. However, in her generalisations she makes the assumption that these primitive societies were devoid of hierarchy, forgetting that, in effect, this has never been the case. Not everyone was magical then, just as not everyone is magical now. And this has little to do with how societies have developed from primitive to industrial. If we are devoid of the knowledge that reminds us of how we can tap into the Ancient Heart, a heart beating faster presumably for the ancients, then it is not because we have forgotten the four principle steps, but because we are coerced into performing meaningless work. But then, back in history, when not everyone was a shaman or a magical person, people also had to perform meaningless work, feeding populations and nurturing growth at the expense of losing some. So what are we comparing? And what are we talking about when we say: 'Let us go back to the ways of the Ancient Heart?'

I find offering secular solutions based on the idea of returns to old cultures designed in accordance with some Romantic vision of the primitive man full of cosmic power as lacking rigor. Magic is a thing for the elect. Shamans of old knew that. Magic chooses people. No matter how much typology and taxonomy and how many reminders we get about how to expand our fields of vision and consciousness, it is not going to help if magic does not elect us. And by 'elect' I don't mean to suggest yet another hierarchy based on essentialism, but rather to describe a state of grace. Election occurs in the moment of listening. 'In the beginning was the pulse, and then the voice of the mother,' contemporary shamans teach us, on just about any weekend spiritual retreat that involves drumming and ecstatic dancing. But it takes a sense of time before history to get there, to experiencing 'the thing itself', the ineffability of the Ancient Heart.

In my own practice of finding magic, I fail. But when I allow magic to find me, I succeed. Before starting writing this essay I was considering the secular solution to the problem of forgetting how to allow the sacred heart to find us in the work proposed by Lynne Kelly on the significance of memory spaces. She defines memory spaces in the following way:

> Memory spaces are simply physical spaces which are visualised as a series of locations. Information you wish to remember can be then added into each location using stories,

puns...anything which makes the link memorable. Once an item of knowledge is linked to the location, any amount of related information can be added. It is not like rote learning. The locations are a framework, a structure much like a database structure into which any amount of information can be added. All cultures which had no contact at all with writing used memory spaces, large and small, to encode their entire knowledge system. Their survival depended on it. (Kelley 2014, Memory Spaces blog)

For instance, Kelly's fascinating work with stone circles advances the argument that such ancient sacred spaces were all built as repositories for passing on knowledge. In her book, *Knowledge and Power in Prehistoric Societies: Orality, Memory and the Transmission of Culture* (2015), she looks at how non-literate cultures stored vast amounts of information about the natural sciences and other practical knowledge. According to her research, the grand pre-historical monuments all constitute a walk in the palace of memory. Every etching tells a story. Every inkling opens doors. Within these stories is encoded some specific knowledge. Her other provocative idea is that these monuments were not merely for ritual and the practice of beliefs, but rather for survival. The knowledge stored in these monuments by way of narrativising all their natural shapes and linking to them specific knowledge about some concrete human activity constituted instruction manuals for living. Indeed, perhaps we can think of Stonehenge or some other stone circle as an ancient self-help book. The question here is: what secular solution to our general problem of disconnectedness can we derive from such research? To what extent can thinking about pre-historic monuments as spaces of memory enhance our understanding of what it means to walk with nature so that we can feel beauty, and hear the Ancient heart say: 'Yes, I'm here now.' As Kelly puts it:

Oral cultures are too often represented on screen and in much academic writing as some kind of quaint primitive creatures who lived in a permanent fog of superstition. If there is a female image, then it is a fertility Goddess. Rituals are nebulous acts, usually interpreted as appeasing Gods, even though many oral cultures don't have Gods who they worship. There is never a mention of formal knowledge systems. There is rarely, if ever, acknowledgement of human intellect, despite us all being the same species. (Memory Spaces blog)

She then goes on to demonstrate how indigenous cultures have sophisticatedly classified and stored knowledge about hundreds of bird and animal species, mappings through songlines, and other such elaborate memory boards as the African lukasas (for instance, the African Luba used such memory boards as mnemonic devices, but only for ritual performed by knowledgeable elders). I find Kelly's work a significant contribution to how we may find it necessary to square off against the culture of typologies, written taxonomies, steps towards improvement, and the marketing mapping of the self.

It is now becoming more acknowledged that ancient cultures had a system for remembering pragmatic information by encoding it in mythology, song, dance, chant, and stories. Each stone can tell a whole story. Each mark on a stone has a mnemonic function. Perhaps what we need is not to figure out how this or that stone can provide us with a four-step programme for storytelling that will align our soul with some new age sensibility, but rather, what we need is to just pay attention. Here I see a parallel between Kelly's work and Murray's work, insofar as they both present us with the possibility to practice being present while making recourse to an enhanced mode of listening to our surroundings. What can we learn from paying attention? My own claim is that through reassessing memory through practice, the practice of listening to our natural environment, and even technology, we come closer to hearing the voice of our ancestors. But this kind of listening can only occur in solitude, in the anonymous space while transiting from one place to another – however mundane or metaphysical – or in the space that invites us to realise that what we all sit on is a large pile of bones. The bones of our ancestors.

Philosopher and culture critic Marc Augé talks about 'functionalised transit places' in his book *Non-Places: Introduction to an Anthropology of Supermodernity* (1995) and makes the point that we only remember spaces such as the airport, or the shopping mall in generic terms. But they do have an impact on our lives nonetheless. Modern culture makes its own imprints on us, and there's memory encoded on every new stone of our creation. But how do we register it? And if we do, how do we know that it's the Ancient Heart speaking through our iPhones? How can we hear the Gods in such transiting spaces, or the ancient sites we visit as tourists or pilgrims? After visiting Stonehenge, what more can we say than: 'Been there, done that, bought the T-shirt?' What can we make of the sacred messages that may reach us in an encounter with the unseen while waiting in line at the cash register to pay for our groceries?

Augé makes the observation that anthropology has always been concerned with the here and now, and that it is precisely the immediacy of the moment that is at odds with the discipline of observing events first-hand and then reflecting on what has been observed, the latter often changing the narrative of the first-hand experience, insofar as it is informed by what conditions the production of the text are based on including the culture of publishing and general prejudice (Augé, 1995: 8). As he puts it:

The term 'historical anthropology' is ambiguous to say the least. 'Anthropological history' seems more appropriate. A symmetrical and inverse example might be found in the way anthropologists – Africanists, for example – are obliged to dip into history, notably in the form it has taken in the oral tradition. Everyone knows Hampaté Ba's dictum that in Africa, and old person dying is 'a library on fire'; but the informant, whether old or not, is someone having a conversation who tells us less about the past than about what he knows or thinks of the past. He is not contemporary with the events he narrates, but the ethnologist is contemporary with both the narrative and the narrator. The informant's account says as much about the present as it does about the past. So, the anthropologist, who has and ought to have historical interests, is nevertheless not *stricto sensu* a historian.

In the context of our discussion here, which tries to account for how we might define the Ancient Heart before we go with it, return to it, or restore it, I find it relevant to note the impasse that historians, reconstructivists, and revisionists find themselves in whenever they have to deal with 'reinventing' actual events surrounding cultures about which we know little. And yet, when looking at such pan revisionist material that the Golden Section Order Society has produced, we clearly get a sense of how this problem of fictionalised narratives in the context of precise location – Stonehenge is pretty fixed – fits the framework in which an argument works by virtue of its obeying the law of symmetrical relations. If a system of correspondence is created, then all it needs in order to be able to account for and explain a particular world-vision is to re-create a relation between the 'now' and the 'here' as it organises itself along the axiom of 'as above, so below'.

Given Kelly's research and Augé's notions of the 'non-place' that equates with where we can locate the Ancient Heart, perhaps we can argue that this relation between the 'now' and the 'here' that some revivalists are conditioned on is the same as the relation in which the narrator's experience of the 'now' – even when the 'now' is historically located in the past – is completely symmetrical with the narrated 'here'. The function of the Ancient Heart in this relation of mediating between the present and the past through acts of the imagination is to provide us with a method of testing personal gnosis. I think that it is precisely in this that I value the work of Colin Murray, as it draws our attention to the traps and challenges in relying too much on what we take for granted from mystery schools. Correspondence is good, but too much of it creates dogma. Mystery schools have been known for creating the most fascinating systems of correspondences, but as Murray suggests, along with critics interested in memory theatres, creating a system of correspondence should not come at the expense of 'seeing'. Rather it should be based on taking a walk, and committing what you see to memory, while creating a corresponding link to the 'thing itself' and the way in which you come to process and understand the information that you receive from experiencing the thing itself. Only in this way can the Ancient Heart be passed down to the ones that come after us. The Ancient Heart is not about what correspondences we can make, but about what we can actually see. The Ancient Heart plays the role of the impenetrable obvious, and because of that remains forever a mystery.

Bibliography

Augé, Marc 1995. *Non-Places: Introduction to an Anthropology of Supermodernity.* Verso, London.

Beck, Martha 2013 (2012). *Finding Your Way in a Wild New World.* London: Atria Books.

Borlace, William 1758. *Observations on the Antiquities Historical and Monumental, of the County of Cornwall. Consisting of Several Essays on the First Inhabitants, Druid-sup.* Gale, Andover.

Jabès, Edmond 1989. *The Book of Shares.* University Press, Chicago.

Kelly, Lynn 2015 (ongoing). *Memory Spaces.*

http://memoryspaces.com.au/ Blog last accessed: Jan. 31, 2105.

Kelly, Lynn 2015. *Knowledge and Power in Prehistoric Societies: Orality, Memory and the Transmission of Culture*. Cambridge University Press, Cambridge.

Murray, Colin 1984. 'Brigantia' in *The New Celtic Review*: 35: February-April. Golden Section Order Society Publication, London.

Tuning into the Landscape

By Sarah Hollingham

I'm sitting on a chair with my fellow Quakers in a wide circle in a field in Suffolk. There's an unspoken need to kick off my shoes and feel the bare ground and the grass between my toes. I sit upright, feet firmly planted down on the ground, hoping to lock into the energy from the earth, my hands are relaxed in my lap. Glancing around the circle at my fellow Friends some have eyes shut, heads back, gazing upwards towards the sun, others heads bowed to their laps. I concentrate on centring down, focusing on my breathing, acknowledging and then dismissing the sounds around me and clearing my mind from those chasing thoughts. Some are difficult to catch and dismiss. I close my eyes and block out all the visual messages: tents, campfire and abandoned children's bicycles near the marquee. The wind brushes my face and moves through my clothes.

Birkell (2004) observes that 'to sit in silence is often to notice how unsilent the world is and unstill one's body is' – how true! I acknowledge one, no two, different birdsongs, a tractor travelling down the lane, the shushed murmurs of children playing on rugs in the centre of our circle. I sit here and accept all these sounds and then try to set them aside. I need my mind to escape from the thought machine, which is still pounding away.

This meeting is towards the end of our Quaker week within a community of Friends, and the connections between us all seem stronger as we have had to resolve our various, often petty, conflicts. Becoming quiet and receptive arrives sooner than expected. I sense something rather special and powerful within our circle as my core arrives at stillness and it appears that I'm not the only one feeling this spirit. By waiting and making space in my head between the usual babble, I'm able to allow a spiritual presence to enter and in this case a spiritual earth presence dominates.

The firm impression that remains within me after this meeting, and one that has grown stronger as our week living under canvas has progressed, is that we are all passing through the landscape, and that we are all part of something much bigger that runs on a different timetable to ours. The fields around me hold the memories of layer upon layer of human influence. From this week away on Quaker camp, the whole concept of the landscape having a much stronger voice, if we choose to hear it, is uppermost in my mind – I am left with a *need* to be outside and feel the elements, rather than being insulated from them.

I begin to question why it is that my experiences of Quaker meeting for worship in this field are so different to my local meeting in a centrally heated room in a community centre. Usually, after centring down, it's a human focus that comes through. For instance, last week at meeting the theme was around truth. Nature didn't get much of a look in.

Does place of worship make this difference, or do the sounds of the landscape that filter through into my subconscious shape the outcome? How can I give nature a voice in my daily life? After all, our ancestors were more attuned to the natural world and would have lived much like us during our week at camp – cooking on a fire, access to only cold water, and the weather having a direct impact on our daily lives. If we go back to pre-Christian times, the Anglo-Saxons would have had a hall central to their community; a place to gather, eat, share stories and entertain, similar to our central marquee at camp. The experience of Quaker camp is far more connected to the rawness of nature and past ways of living than our everyday lives where there is the tendency to retreat into a virtual world of new technologies, remote from other people.

Quaker meeting provides a means of silent worship where, if we can commit ourselves and reach a level of stillness, we find that a spiritual presence can transform us and, if rightly followed, will lead us into unity and love. Quaker *testimonies* stem from this concept. The Quaker use of *Advice and Queries* (1995) is flexible and is a source of both challenge and inspiration to Friends in our personal lives, because being a Quaker is not just about attending a weekly meeting for worship, it is a lifestyle based around *Equality, Peace, Simplicity and Truth*. One such example is number 42 from *Advice and Queries* that states:

> We do not own the world, and its riches are not ours to dispose of at will. Show a loving consideration for all creatures, and seek to maintain the beauty and variety of the world. Work to ensure that our increasing 'power over' nature is used responsibly, with reverence for life…

For me, it was this statement that held greatest prominence in my mind after a week at camp.

A fellow Friend told me that his year starts from Quaker Camp as this daily outside meeting for worship helps him to reflect upon the previous year and readdress the balance in his life. The main concept with which I left camp this year was to find some greater connection with the earth, so that when I centre down to find stillness, the space is filled with a greater spiritual presence of the natural world – an earth spirit – to guide my actions within it.

The next stage in my spiritual journey to reach a more balanced equilibrium between my lifestyle and the natural world came a month later, when a friend invited me to camp in her wood, a ten-acre ancient woodland in the depths of East Kent.

Using the sat nav on my phone, I found a route down to Kent. As I drove I pondered why it was that the one map that most people use – whether it be via Google maps or a paper version – is a road map; the 'vital' blood vessels criss-crossing our country, stacked in ancient history.

Way points have ancient names whose natural features have long dissolved into the land. But there is no detail, no way to know where I can access the countryside. Our roads are so busy and it seems unwise to just pull over. Our land laws are so strict and each acre of land belongs to someone else. Is this why it seems harder to immerse ourselves in the landscape? It's incredible that even my methods of navigation seem to distance me from what I'm trying to seek a greater connection with. At this point, the human imprint on our landscape appears far stronger to me than any natural process.

After driving for a few hours, the roads become gradually smaller and quieter. Margaret has already unlocked the gate and parked her van in the woody glade. As I drive in, the peacefulness wraps round me like a comforting cloak and is in sharp contrast to the constant hum of engine and road noise that accompanied me throughout my journey.

My car looks like it has arrived from some distant planet. It sits rather uncomfortably on the clay soil fearful of going any further into the wood. The wheels would sink into the mud that is there all the year round where overhanging trees shade the ride. Abandoning my car and walking in, I feel as if the wood is watching me. This privately owned wood has a very different feel to my local grove on the edge of my hometown.

The wood is perfectly self-sufficient – there is no public access here to disturb the way of life. Nature rules in this little pocket of Kent sandwiched between the motorways and busyness; plants along the paths are not used to trampling, they are enjoying the extra sunlight and are a mass of diversity with leaves of multiple shapes, colours and designs. History is stored in the seed bank in the soil, a distant trace back to the ancient woodland and the wildwood heritage. Seeds lay dormant for years in the soil beneath my feet, only being liberated when the micro-climate and soil conditions are right.

Woodland is a complete ecosystem, able to fend for herself –

a mosaic of different habitats. She has a story to tell. Am I seeing this wood as early inhabitants had? In Anglo Saxon times woodland management and timber were at the heart of their society. Here there are sections of previously coppiced chestnut with the odd majestic oak reaching up to the canopy and knarled old and twisted hornbeams all seeded in a different age. This pattern of wood being managed to provide underwood and timber speaks of our ancestors. Rackman (1994) explains how underwood was produced by coppicing, where the tree was felled and allowed to grow again from the stumps to provide successive crops of rods and poles, used for many purposes: wattle-and-daub, fencing and especially for fuel. Scattered among the underwood stools were timber trees, allowed to stand for thirty years or more and then felled to make beams and planks. Underwood can be from a variety of species, but timber was predominately oak – so perhaps what I am seeing here is just as it would have been many centuries ago.

In relation to finding the story behind our landscape, I think W.G. Hoskins was right when he declared: 'One needs to be a botanist, a physical geographer, and a naturalist, as well as a historian, to be able to feel certain that one has all the facts right before allowing the imagination to play over the small details of a scene.' Robert MacFarlane (2007) observed in his book *Wild Places*: 'Every islet and mountain-top, every secret valley or woodland, has been visited, dwelled in, worked, or marked at some point in the past five millennia. The human and the wild cannot be partitioned.' It's this layer upon layer of human influence on our landscape, the legacy of past peoples working the landscape, that shows how my visit is only a tiny speck in relation to the age of the trees around me.

This aspect of trees operating on a different timescale than us is evident with oaks. Trees are not immortal as Rackham (2006) is keen to point out and interestingly management techniques, such as pollarding and coppicing, can extend a tree's life to at least 800 years. One such tree is 'Old Knobbley' in Essex. This is an oak with its own website and Facebook page and was runner up in the Woodland Trust's Tree of the Year competition. Old Knobbley is a clear illustration of how our life on earth is just a small part of that of a tree and that over the centuries, this particular tree has been harvested for timber by pollarding and is another element that links us to our own ancestral story.

Unless I unravel these layers of time recorded in the vegetation and ground features around me, like Oliver Rackham did in his study of Hayley Wood, my experience of Margaret's wood is going to be like a chaotic symphony – a mass of sounds, beautiful or impressive, but without the analysis of each rhythm or melody. So whatever means I develop for my personal connection with the landscape, this can only be a starting point and will probably open up more questions than answers. Unless, of course, my focus is on the process itself of tuning in and reaching a sense of mindfulness and stillness in order for a spiritual voice from the earth to be heard.

However, as I bed down for the night in a clearing within the wood, I feel disconnected and uncomfortable with the wildness around me. Margaret had chosen her usual camping spot where there is only room for one tent, and I am alone in my attempts to adjust to the music of rustling of leaves, twigs breaking, scuttling of tiny feet across the ground, flutter of wings and calls from this unaccustomed night life around me. With a job in an environmental office, I like to think that I don't live an entirely urban lifestyle, but maybe I am cut off from the wider natural world as it's very rare that I get the opportunity to 'wild camp'. Screaming when I saw a snake earlier in the day was probably a good indication of my detachment. The complete darkness that wrapped around me and the multitude of sounds are unsettling.

Belton (2014) writes: 'It is nothing short of tragic that children deprived of an early introduction to nature should feel fear at the sight of lofty trees and twinkling stars rather than in awe and wonder which would nourish the spirit.'

Although I hate to admit it, maybe this applies to me too. I need to open up and relax rather than fight the differences that have taken me out of my comfort zone. I need to find a way in to understanding my role within the natural world and then locate it in the geography of me and my *sense of place*. After all, we can't protect and look after something if we are unable to love and understand it. Unlike many civilisations before me, or even farmers or foresters today, I'm not in the situation where the land is at the heart of my existence.

Over the course of the weekend, by immersing myself in the wood away from all modern facilities, I become one step closer in finding a way to connect with the ancestral landscape. A key part of this reconnection is a snippet of a conversation over twenty years earlier that came into focus again. The old warden of Headley Heath, in Surrey, taught me the value of stopping everything that you are doing and just listening. Not chatting, not thinking – just listening. This 'stopping everything your doing' is a bit like the start of a Quaker meeting, where I listen, accept sounds then put them to one side to make space for a spiritual presence. So I pick my way between the brambles away from comfort of the central ride and I explore much deeper into the body of the wood.

The path in front of me is consensual in form without common care or common practice – it has almost disappeared, overgrown by vegetation. Looking back, I see no footprints. Here I stand and here I listen.

The location or geography of sounds that we hear in the landscape are all products of our ancestry, for we are not living in a truly 'wild' landscape. There are reasons behind why a road is located in a specific place – perhaps it was to follow field boundaries, or maybe a local dispute changed the planned route, or else the improvements of ancient Roman culture upon the landscape determined the road's course. Geography also explains why

settlements are located where they are – the river for trans-
porting food and water, a main road for trading, hills for ritual
use or for defence against flooding and so on. Features of the
landscape shaped by humanity, and the subsequent management
of them, also affect the geography of the *sounds* that we hear.

So, to progress my journey further, I sought to explore sound
and find a quicker way to tune in that I could use in my daily life.
I seek to develop this process of stopping, listening and purely
focusing on sound in order to still my mental thought machine
and fulfil my need to reconnect more fully to the landscape – my
sense of place and my inner wellbeing. This contrasts to the
popular view of a natural landscape and the importance of its
aesthetic qualities – a pretty view, a panorama – something that
would make a great photo. In order to show a loving consideration for all creatures and seek to maintain the beauty and
variety of the world, we need to use all of our senses, not just
sight. Sound can go deeper. Sound enables us to immerse
ourselves in the 'here and now' and bring that into
consciousness, rooting ourselves into the ground beneath our
feet. In the past a comprehensive knowledge of the soundscape
was crucial to survival. Today we block out the soundscape with
headphones or else let it wash over us unnoticed. By developing
our ability to listen we can learn to let the soundscape seep
deeply into our subconscious, in much the same way as I had
during the outside meeting for worship at Quaker camp. The
ancestral landscape can then have a stronger voice within us.

As a geographer, mapping is part of me. Harman (2004) has
put together a fascinating book, collecting different types of
creative map and points out that: 'Mapmaking fulfils one of our
deepest desires: understanding the world around us and our
place in it.' The art of mapmaking and the process of mapping
something ephemeral and invisible like sound is rather special. It
ignores the standard mapping conventions of scale and gridlines
and is a truly personal viewpoint and interpretation. Sounds of

the natural world remind us that there is another world out there beyond our human one, one in which our own concerns and worries take on a smaller size and seem more manageable. This concept of seeing beyond our own world proves beneficial in lots of ways.

To map sound, sit or stand with paper and pen and imagine your location as the centre of the page. Devise symbols, shapes, lines and marks to indicate the direction of the sound if it is moving, or the location of the sound in relation to you. For instance, sounds behind us may be drawn at the bottom of the page, in front of us at the top of the page and left and right respectively. Some marks may also indicate the feel of the sound especially if it is the wind as it ebbs and flows. Within this process, do not take much heed to guidebooks or field guides, so different birdsongs may be marked as bird 1, bird 2 etc.

This process is available to everyone and that's key here because it's the listening and mapping process rather than the outcome (the map), that is important. The map created just serves as a record of what has been heard and a reminder of the feelings that were experienced.

On the surface this creative soundmapping process seems pretty straightforward, but like a Quaker meeting it's surprisingly hard to discard the babble of thoughts churning around in the brain and focus solely on sound. So, after visiting Margaret's wood and coming back into my world of parenting, working and all those day-to-day stresses, I decided to map sound for a month and not to travel anywhere special. So, I had no excuses not to map or just to make time in my day for mapping my normal routes and outdoor spaces. Mapping sound in my garden showed: birdsongs, doors slamming, traffic, rhythmic barking of a dog and swirling wind. From this starting point the sound maps became more sophisticated in the expressions I used.

The mechanical process of putting pen to paper helps me to block out unwanted distractions and connect. This soundmapping soon develops into a type of meditation and has restorative power. How much time do I give to stopping and listening to the world around me? It is rather worrying for the future of our natural world, as I am not alone in my busy lifestyle, this cycle of insulating myself from the outside world. I'm beginning to realise it takes effort to come off this treadmill of busy modern life and unless I make an effort to listen to the landscape around me, it will never reach my subconscious and link with something deeper.

The first challenge is mapping the interaction between the human and natural world and the mosaic of birdsong, dogs barking, traffic, and wind interweaving everything together – all sounds influenced by how the land is used, whether hedgerow, allotment or field.

In 1801 Burnett (1986) estimated that: 'Around 80 per cent of the population of England and Wales was still 'rural' and some 20 per cent 'urban' [with urban] defined as living in towns having more than 5,000 inhabitants.' Today these percentages are switched over and around 80 per cent of us live in urban areas. Our landscape is very different to that of our ancestors, although our human need to connect to our countryside has in no way diminished. After all, being a good listener is at the heart of a fulfilling relationship. We don't need to be in middle of a field in rural Suffolk or the in the middle of an ancient woodland to feel a link with the land. This country isn't a wild landscape, and everything within the soundscape is related to people (and vice versa). If we provide opportunities, nature will find a space alongside.

During the process of sound mapping, we reach a point of stillness with the added benefit of reducing our stress levels. One such occasion was going out along my usual lunchtime walk, through a shabby urban park near my office. On previous sound maps I found that once I had quietened my busy thoughts from racing around, there was a lot of different birdsong and it demonstrated that even the scraggy line of trees and scrub had an ecological value. On this particular occasion I had been trying all morning to unravel the conflicting interests around a complex site at work. I stood with my page open and pen at the ready, then I realised that I couldn't hear any birdsong or any trees rustling as my thoughts were so loud and prominent, whirling away problem solving. I had to turn down the volume in my head so I could hear what was around me and this took about ten minutes or so. It was a conscious process. To my amazement, once I was able to tune the dial my stress eased and I started to map.

My hearing hadn't suddenly improved. These sounds were always there. I just couldn't hear them as my mind was disconnected to the landscape around me. In the same way, we can walk along the street wearing headphones and, after a while, the music washes over and you miss the lyrics. By taking off our headphones, whether they are actual or virtual, and tuning in, we will find that nature becomes much closer and that experience can have restorative powers. A fine antidote, perhaps, to our fast-paced technology-driven lives, showing that our lives can indeed become a different and a more spiritually nourishing experience for us.

Sitting on a chair with my fellow Quaker Friends in a wide circle in a field in Suffolk, there's an unspoken need to kick off my shoes and feel the bare ground and the grass between my toes. The stillness of this circle reveals, not silence, but a landscape full of sound and full of life influenced by our forebears – a rainbow of harmony that is ancestral, ever-present and very much alive.

Bibliography

1995. *Quaker Faith and Practice*. Yearly Meeting of the Religious Society of Friends in Britain. Euston, London.

Belton, Teresa 2014. *Happier People, Healthier Planet*. Silver Wood Books, Bristol.

Birkel, Michael, Lawrence 2004. *Silence and Witness: The Quaker Tradition.* Darton, Longman and Todd, London.

Burnett, John 1986. *A Social History of Housing 1815-1985.* Routledge, London.

Harmon, Katherine 2004. *You are Here: Personal Geographies and Other Maps of the Imagination.* Princeton Architectural Press, New York.

Hoskins, William, George 1955 (1985). *The Making of the English Landscape.* Penguin, London.

MacFarlane, Robert 2007. *The Wild Places.* Granta, London.

Old Knobbley available from: http://www.oldknobbley.com/ (Accessed 24 December 2014)

Rackham, Oliver 1975. *Hayley Wood, It's History and Ecology.* Cambridge & Isle of Ely Naturalists' Trust Ltd, Cambridge.

Rackham, Oliver 1994. *Trees and Woodland in Anglo-Saxon England: The Documentary Evidence.* Council for British Archaeology. York.

Rackham, Oliver 2006. *Woodlands.* New Naturalist Library, Harper and Collins, London.

Southall, Joseph, Edward 2006. *Silence.* Quaker Outreach Leaflet, Euston, London.

How Genetics Unravels the Role of the Landscape in the Relationship Between Ancestors and Present

By Luzie U Wingen

Introduction

Genetics can be a means of understanding natural processes, which in turn helps us to understand the relationships between ancestors, landscape and living species. The term *genetics* will be used in the sense of it being a scientific field that strives to understand questions like: 'How are individuals linked to their ancestors?' or 'Why do individuals partly look like their ancestors and partly not?' and 'Why is each individual unique?' and so on. Here, I will share with you the insights that we have into the genetic history of different species, and specifically human, oak and wheat. Moreover, I will explain how genetic history can inform us about the natural forces that help shape each individual, and then introduce you to some modern genetic techniques that have helped us in gaining that insight.

Basic principles of genetics

Human beings, like all other organisms, inherit traits from their parents and pass them on to their children. This inheritance is brought about by the genes each organism carries, which are manifested in *DNA*. DNA are large complex organic molecules, composed of four different sub-units, the *nucleotides* A, C, G and T. For one DNA molecule, many of these nucleotides are organised in a strand of **double helix** configuration. In general, all cells of an organism contain a specific number of DNA strands, organised into *chromosomes*. Each chromosome contains one DNA molecule. The secret of the DNA lies in the sequence of units. The genetic information is stored in this sequence and is thus the *genetic memory* of the cell or the organism. The genetic information contains the instruction of how to *build* the organism, how to keep it *functional* and how to *reproduce*. For the sake of briefness, I will mainly talk about reproduction here, as this is of major relevance in understanding the genetic history and the link between ancestors and extant (existing) species. However, this does not mean that other functions of the DNA are less important... It is of the utmost importance for the organism to keep the information content correct and in a good state. This process of organisation could be compared to a cook book that contains old recipes that are passed on from one generation to the next. In order for the instructions to be understood, all pages need to be present and in the right order. Returning to the genetic information, *cellular mechanisms protect* the DNA in order to safeguard the information that instructs the cell processes for present and future generations. During reproduction, the genetic information of the parents is passed on to the child. If the complete genetic information is passed on without any changes, each of the children will be genetically identical to the parent. This is, for example, the case when a spider plant develops plantlets on its extended stems. This type of producing progeny is called *asexual* reproduction.

However, this is not what is generally observed in the plant and animal world. Instead, *sexual reproduction* is common in most flora and fauna. In the process of sexual reproduction, the genetic material of two individuals of the same species is combined. As a result, progenies have new combinations of the genetic information of both parents and have more *diverse* characteristics. Just by chance, some of the progenies might have a combination of genetic material that makes them better suited for the parental environment, or even for a different environment, in which the parents have not managed to prosper. This strategy makes the species as a whole less vulnerable to changing environmental conditions. In other cases it helps a species to better adapt to an existing environment and to be more successful than others. As a side effect of the sexual recombination, an initial *reduction of the genetic material* has to occur. That is what happens in the formation of egg and sperm cells, and similarly within the carpel of the flower and in the pollen. If reduction of genetic material would not take place before egg and sperm merge, the amount of genetic material would be duplicated each time an organism reproduces, and soon enough there would be no more space in the cell for anything else than genetic material and all other cell processes would cease. Instead, a reduction to one full set of genes, the so-called *genome* occurs. During the reduction process, a random exchange of genetic material between the two genome sets present occurs. This process is known as *genetic assortment*.

Two such re-assorted sets or genomes are then combined in the process of sexual reproduction, and form a *diploid genome* (double set). As a result of the many possible combinations of parental genetic information, each new organism formed via sexual reproduction has a unique combination of the genetic information. In my opinion, this genetic uniqueness informs, in part, *identity* in humans and other species.

Genetic techniques

The human interest in genetic principles goes back a long time. It probably arose when early humans observed that animals or plants produced offspring that looked very much like their parents. We can assume that a basic understanding of genetic principles was present when hunter-gathers learned how to farm and how to domesticate useful species. They started to breed animals and plants by selecting individuals for preferred *traits*, and by interbreeding the individuals with those favourable traits. Our understanding has increased since then, initially by the discovery of the laws called *Mendelian inheritance* (Mendel 1866). Mendel first deduced these laws from observations on easily distinguishable traits in parents and progeny in experimental crosses in garden peas.

Following that, scientist learned how to study the genetic information directly. As stated previously, the genetic information of two parents is different and every individual is unique. The differences may only concern specific DNA regions, also called genetic *loci*, which are in specific states. The specific state of a genetic locus is called an *allele*. The difference in state would be due to a different DNA sequence, often different by a very small variation. Modern molecular genetic techniques allow geneticists to determine such differences.

Initially only a low number of loci per chromosome could be investigated, or *genotyped*, as the process was time consuming and expensive. Following on from the genotyping, the process of *genetic mapping* puts the genetic loci into the correct chromosomal order. In recent decades these techniques have undergone massive improvements and have become cheaper and much faster. Genetic mapping is now ultimately refined in the technique of *genetic sequencing*, by which the state of every single nucleotide of the total DNA strand is revealed. The sequences of a large number of people have been identified. This means that the knowledge concerning the genetic differences within a population of humans is currently one of the most in-depth studied. However, individuals of many other species have also been sequenced, and for many more species at least some basic genetic characterisation has been conducted. In this way, the knowledge of the ancestry of the individuals studied has been largely revealed.

Landscape genetics

As a result of the rapid development of methods to characterise and understand genetic information, it became feasible to investigate genetic trends of whole populations instead of focussing on single individuals. Understanding the genetics of populations is more important for the research into evolutionary principles. There are different evolutionary forces that work on populations. Some forces are directed, e.g. in a climate cooling phase before an ice-age, those individuals in a population will have an advantage that are more cold tolerant. These individuals will as a result be stronger and have more progenies. As a result, the genetic composition of the future population will be different from the current one and will have higher frequencies of alleles coming from those cold-tolerant individuals. Other forces are non-selective or random, e.g. due to a natural catastrophe such as a landslide, or a particular tree population might be wiped out in spite of being perfectly adapted to the habitat. This means that, in spite of being strong and healthy, their genes will not make it into the future generation. Having progenies means the genetic information will be passed on to the next generation and will contribute to future populations.

Geneticists realised, however, that genetic processes cannot be fully understood just by analysing allele numbers outside the context of the landscape. This insight gave rise to the field of *landscape genetics* (Manel 2003), the approach of which aims to understand how geographical and environmental features structure genetic variation at both population and individual levels. The landscape plays a major role in the process of evolution, as Darwin and Wallace discovered (1858). Darwin's example is of the Galapagos finches – different but related bird species, each confined to different islands. All of these birds seem to be derived from one common ancestor, but each species has a different beak shape, perfectly adapted to the food sources found on their respective islands. The explanation for the variety of species is that the situation of the islands provide separate habitats, leading to genetic specialisation. The distance between the islands made an exchange of genetic material between birds difficult or impossible, and this led to the development of different species. The situation is different on a continuous landmass where, in general, the exchange of genetic material is possible. This means that individuals stay closely related to one another due to the constant exchange, and the formation of species happens infrequently. The Galapagos finches therefore demonstrate the importance of the landscape as an evolutionary factor. However, this also means that already on shorter time scales the landscape is important in influencing the dynamics of populations. It can thus be concluded that the landscape has played an important role in the shaping of any individual, human, animal or plant. The landscape has influenced the genetic composition of the populations that the individual stems from and, going further back in time, the landscape has played a role in selecting, naturally, which individuals were able to pass their genes on to following generations, thereby selecting which individuals will develop to be the ancestors of the future.

The three following examples of oak, human and wheat populations provide insight into how landscape factors have shaped the genetic structure of extant populations.

Oak population structure in Europe

Northern Europe was covered by ice during the last glacial maximum in the Pleistocene, about 26,000-15,000 years ago. Permafrost covered much of the landscape south of the ice-sheet in Northern and Western Europe. Most trees and other plants did not survive under these conditions, and were thus missing from the Northern European landscape when the ice retreated, but some plants with special characteristics were able to survive in small populations in these northerly regions along with some animals (see Bhagwat and Willis 2008 and references therein). This would have been the case for hardy trees with light seeds, including pine and birch, which then were among the first tree species to claim back Northern Europe when the ice retreated. However, most species had to make their comeback from further south from refugia in Italy, and on the Balkan and Spanish peninsulas. For the four European white oak species (*Quercus petraea, Q. robur, Q. pubescens and Q. pyrenaica*), the most important refugia for the re-colonisation of Western Europe and the British Isles was Spain (Dumolin-Lapégue 1997). In comparison to birch, the oak re-colonisation was a slow process. Unlike birch, which has small wind dispersed seeds, oaks have heavy fruits and rely on animals, particularly jays, for their acorn dispersal. However, estimates of colonisation time, deduced from the average distances that jays normally carry acorns, predicted an even slower process of re-colonisation. Rare long-distance dispersal events may explain the higher speed of re-colonisation of the European continent with oaks by 5000 BC (Higgins et al., 2003). A possible example for such a rare event might be the transportation of an acorn inside a squirrel body by a predator.

Landscape barriers, such as mountains or seas, are important for the process of re-colonisation. For European re-colonisation, the Pyrenees, the Alps and the English Channel were all barriers. The opening of the English Channel after the ice age meant that several tree species could not return to the British Isles and establish themselves. Hence, the number of indigenous trees in Britain is lower than on the European continent and only two of the four European oak species, sessile oak (*Q. petraea*) and pendunculate oak (*Q. robur*), made their comeback to Britain as a native plant (Elwes and Henry, 1906). Moreover, although we see the influence of the English Channel as strongest, other barriers will have shaped routes and affected the progress of colonisation, and thus left some kind of genetic trace in that population. For example, early arrivals of species will have had an advantage over later arrivals. Depending on how big the time difference was it would have given early trees the chance to fill most of the available space, and later trees would not be able to get much share of that space. This led to the newly established woods being dominated by one particular type. Geneticist talk here about *a genetic signature*, brought about by these processes of re-colonisation, as the genotype of that one early arrival would be more abundant than those of the others. Such genetic signatures can be found in extant oak populations. The genetic analysis reveals that the genetic diversity of oaks in Europe is highest in Spain where the species survived the cold period. Diversity degrades with the distance from this refugium and is particularly low in Britain. To a lesser extent the shape of the landscape also has an influence on the composition of tree populations. European valley floors tend to contain more diverse tree populations than the slopes of the valley, all due to the way the trees colonised that habitat or landscape.

Closing the circle, not only has the landscape had an influence on the species population, but the populations also have an influence on the landscape. There were fewer founder trees colonising Britain and that has led to forests having less diverse, different tree compositions than in other Northern European regions. This has further consequences on other species, plants and animals, as the landscape is not static but a dynamic ecosystem. As one example, the most famous spring flower in British woodlands is the bluebell, often present in impressively large stands. Bluebell carpets are less known in other Northern European woodlands, where different flowers grow in similar types of wooded landscape.

Human population structure in Europe

Most readers will be familiar with the fact that the origin of humans, including the modern humans, *Homo sapiens*, is in Africa (Veeramah and Hammer 2014). From Africa, humans migrated to other continents. The initial human colonisation of Europe happened approximately 45,000 years ago, coming from the Middle East. This colonisation was followed by retraction to the Southern European refugia during the last glacial maximum, 26,000-15,000 years ago, towards the end of the Paleolithic period, followed by the re-colonisations from the refugia northwards. A third colonisation happened when farming cultures moved into Europe during the Neolithic period 9,000-6,000 years ago. A genetic signature of this third colonisation can still be detected in the DNA of modern-day humans (Veeramah and Hammer 2014). Analysis reveals that Northern Europeans have a closer genetic link to the hunter-gather societies, whereas Southern Europeans share more genetic similarities to the incoming Neolithic farmer societies. This has been revealed by the comparison of DNA from modern and ancient humans. It is quite striking that these two signatures can still be found in modern humans. The most likely reason for this is that the original migration event was very strong and directed, and thus left a strong signature, which survives until today. As agriculture developed in very few locations worldwide (Vavilov 1951), there was a strong direction in this migration, coming from one centre of agriculture in the Fertile Crescent and moving into regions that were unfarmed. The distances covered were large, which meant that the migration took a considerable time over several tens of generations. Due to sexual contact between incoming cultures and local people, the following generations were mixtures between both populations.

The presence of genetic signatures, like the one above, does not mean that there are large genetic differences between individuals from Northern and Southern Europe. Small differences can be detected, but all humans do share a common ancestry. Surprisingly, the common ancestors for Europeans are generally much less distant than assumed. Most Europeans are actually distant cousins, related to one another via a vast network of relationships, as demonstrated by Ralph and Coop (2013). Human relationships over the past 3,000 years were studied by analysing the DNA of modern-day humans from different European countries. By counting the long stretches of DNA that are shared between pairs of individuals, the numbers of common genetic ancestors have been deduced. This, of course, required the knowledge of genetic principles that stem from the processes of how genes are passed on from one generation to the next. It is surprising to see that even individuals from opposite ends of Europe share hundreds of common ancestors. Although there is this large degree of commonality across Europe, there are also striking regional differences. South-Eastern Europeans, for example, share large numbers of common ancestors that date roughly to the era of the Slavic and Hunnic expansions around 1,500 years ago, while most common ancestors Italians share with other populations lived longer than 2,500 years ago. For Britain, two major trends of ancestry can be detected, one shared with the Irish and one with the Germans (Ralph and Coop, 2013).

Wheat population structure in Europe

Bread wheat (*Triticum aestivum*) was domesticated about 10,000 years ago in the Fertile Crescent, which is a region in Western Asia and the Nile Delta in North Africa. Regions in modern-day Anatolia in South-East Turkey were the probable cradle of this important crop plant, which is the product of hybridisations between three different wild grasses (Shewry, 2009). The domestication took place in several steps from wild grasses to a domesticated crop. Wheat can no longer thrive in the wild, as is the case for other domesticated crops, and is dependent on human agriculture for its spread and survival. The process of wheat domestication was most likely guided by human selection and propagation of plants with useful traits. Wheat spread into Europe from Anatolia to Greece (8000 BP) and then both northwards through the Balkans to the Danube (7000 BP) and across to Italy, France and Spain (7000 BP), finally reaching Britain and Scandinavia by about 5000 BP (Shewry 2009). The spread of wheat happened at a moderate speed. The slowness can be explained by the necessity of the farming societies to develop locally adapted varieties, called *landraces*, for regions that differed significantly from the origin or from the previous region the farmers had come from. In many cases regional adaptation was necessary in order to develop varieties that were able to prosper in more distant and different environments.

The adaptation was achieved by *breeding*, selecting the best performing lines and crossing these with one another to achieve better adapted landrace varieties. As climate and other environmental conditions are very different between South-East Turkey and Northern Europe, many such steps of local adaptation had to be performed in order to have well yielding crops in all these locations. This process, again, has left a genetic signature behind. The genetic analysis of landraces from *ancestral wheat* collections has identified at least five ancestral European groups (Wingen 2014). The differences in daylight conditions between geographic regions are one example of an important factor in the adaptation process. The Fertile Crescent, being close to the equator, has little variation in day length. In contrast, there is roughly an eight hours difference of day length between summer and winter in Northern Europe. A plant species has to flower at the right time in order to find the optimum conditions to produce seeds or fruits. For wheat, that meant that it had to use different environmental cues in Northern Europe than in the Fertile Crescent.

Interestingly, it has been shown that in line with this observed daylight difference, genes that control the daylight response in wheat were found to be in different states depending on the region the varieties came from (Fjellheim 2014). Other conditions, such as altitude or the likelihood of drought, required other combinations of traits to best yield in a specific environment. In this way, even the human-selected wheat crop is very much adapted to the landscape if we include diverse environmental conditions in this term. At the same time, all wheat plants are derived from the same distant ancestors in the Fertile Crescent. However, landraces from one region are closer related to one another, than those from different geographic regions. Therefore, the genetic composition of a landrace is brought about by a combination of factors. There were random elements, e.g. the route the plants came to a location, and selective elements, where plants were chosen that yielded highest. Due to parts of the process having been non-selective it is possible to improve landraces by breeding. There may be alleles present in distant landraces that confer a higher yield or disease resistance or other advantageous traits, which have not made it into a specific landrace. This is one reason that the modern elite lines, carefully bred for higher diversity, have replaced landraces in Britain and many other countries with modern agriculture. Modern wheat varieties are frequently grown in large monocultures of a very limited set of varieties. However, a recent trend in agronomy partly addresses the landscape factor more strongly again. The method of *Precision Farming* assesses on-farm soil and environmental conditions to a high degree or precision. With this knowledge, the potential of each field or even part of a field can be determined. In accordance with this knowledge, potential crop varieties are chosen that best fit those conditions. This means, for example, that it is more economical to plant low-input varieties on sandy soils, as fertiliser would run off quickly. The low-input varieties will yield less than high-input, high-performing lines, however the costs for inefficient fertiliser input can be avoided. The on-farm diversity regarding the number of different varieties used is, as a result, much higher in Precision Farming than in the monocultural style of farming. Here, the link between landscape and variety is human choice and not natural selection.

The process of adapting crops to the environment is not at an endpoint. Wheat breeding is currently still achieving small increases in wheat yields and the work on breeding and adapting crops to environments is of high importance due to climate change as result of global warming.

Conclusions

What do genetics teach us about ancestors? We know, that ancestors are *survivors*, otherwise they would not have modern relatives, but would be extinct lineages or species. However, does 'survivor' mean that they were stronger than other individuals at that time? Not necessarily. Some of them were surely stronger, others might have been more flexible when conditions changed, or more *co-operative* to survive as a group. Many were just lucky; they were at the right place at the right time. The ancestors made the best out of the situation they were in. The landscape had, and still has, a strong influence on which individuals contribute to the following generation. The influence is partly directed when there is an advantage for individuals in a population with a certain trait. The influence of landscape may also be without direction or a random phenomenon. So, ancestors were partly better than average, partly co-operative and partly lucky, which sounds like a good mixture to me. We are survivors, but partly due to fortune.

Bibliography

Bhagwat, Shonil. A. and Willis, Katherine. J. 2008. 'Species Persistence in Northerly Glacial Refugia of Europe: A Matter of Chance or Biogeographical Traits?' in *Journal of Biogeography* 35:464–482.

Darwin, Charles and Wallis, Alfred, Russell July 1st 1858. 'On the Tendency of Species to form Varieties; and on the Perpetuation of Varieties and Species by Natural Means of Selection' in *Proceedings of the Linnean Society of London*. London.

Dumolin-Lapégue, S., Demesure, B., Fineschi, S., Le Corre, V., and Petit, R. J. 1997. 'Phylogeographic Structure of White Oaks Throughout the European Continent' in *Genetics* 146:1475–1487.

Elwes, Henry, John and Henry, Augustine 1906. *The Trees of Great Britain & Ireland*. Privately printed in Edinburgh.

Fjellheim, S., Boden, S. and Trevaskis, B. 2014. 'The Role of Seasonal Flowering Responses in Adaptation of Grasses to Temperate Climates' in *Frontiers in Plant Science* 5, 431. doi:10.3389/fpls.2014.00431.

Higgins, S. I., Nathan, R. and Cain, M. L. 2003. 'Are Long-distance Dispersal Events in Plants Usually Caused by Non-standard Means of Dispersal' in *Ecology* 84:1945–1956.

Manel, S., Schwartz, Michael, K., Luikart, G., and Taberlet, P. 2003. 'Landscape Genetics: Combining Landscape Ecology and Population Genetics' in *Trends in Ecology and Evolution* 18(4):189–197.

Mendel, Gregor 1866. 'Versuche über Pflanzen-Hybriden' in *Verhandlungen des naturforschenden Vereines in Brünn* 4:3–47.

Ralph, Peter and Coop, Graham 2013. 'The Geography of Recent Genetic Ancestry Across Europe' in *PLoS Biology* 11(5):e1001555.

Shewry, Peter, R. 2009. 'Wheat' in *Journal of Experimental Botany* 60:1537–1553.

Vavilov, Nikolai, Ivanovich 1951 (trans. by Doris Love). *Origin and Geography of Cultivated Plants* University Press, Cambridge.

Veeramah, Krishna, R. and Hammer, Michael. F. 2014. 'The impact of whole-genome sequencing on the reconstruction of human population history' in *Nature Reviews Genetics*, 15(3):149–162.

Wallace, Alfred, Russel 1858. 'On the Tendency of Varieties to Depart Indefinitely From the Original Type' in *Proceedings of the Linnean Society of London* 53–62.

Wingen, Luzie U., Orford, S., Goram, R., Leverington-Waite, M., Bilham, L., Patsiou, T. S., Ambrose, M., Dicks, J. and Griffiths, S. 2014.' Establishing the A. E. Watkins Landrace Cultivar Collection as a Resource for Systematic Gene Discovery in Bread Wheat' in *Theoretical and Applied Genetics* 127(8):1831–1842.

Glossary

BP: Before present.

DNA: Deoxyribonucleic acid, a molecule that encodes the genetic sequence. A succession of letters that indicates the order of nucleotides G, A, C, T.

Allele: The specific state or form of a gene, e.g. maternal and paternal allele.

Gene: The molecular unit of heredity of a living organism.

Genome: The total complement of genes, or the complete genetic material, in an organism or cell.

Genetic Locus: The specific location of a gene on a chromosome. The plural is loci.

Haploid: A cell that contains one set of chromosomes. Sperm or egg cells are haploid.

Diploid: A cell that contains two sets of chromosomes, usually one from the mother and one from the father.

SNP: A Single Nucleotide Polymorphism (pronounced snip) is a DNA sequence variation occurring commonly within a population. A single nucleotide (A, T, C or G) in the genome differs between members of that population.

Landrace: A domesticated, locally adapted, traditional variety of a domesticated crop species.

Evolution: The change in heritable phenotype traits of biological populations over successive generations. Evolutionary processes give rise to diversity at every level of biological organisation, including the level of species, individual organisms, and at the level of molecular evolution.

Ancestors (Anck-est-ors)

By David Loxley

A traditional interpretation of the word 'ancestor' leads us to its present tense meaning. Ancestors leave behind material objects to remind us of who they were, these objects and words represent our relationship with the past, which for the most part is a dead past. Trees are nourished by the leaves they drop to the earth. If we want to resurrect our ancestors as immortal we need to let go of our beliefs – of who we think we are. We need to ask questions that can pass through the wall we have built between life and death that will maintain our aliveness to our distant inheritance. We share the present tense with our ancestors, but we have become separated.

Language

The condition of language is not as we might think it is. The formation of language, like everything else in the universe, emerged from nothing, from somewhere else outside of us. The English dictionary that we use is based mainly on Latin and Greek and is mostly translated into meanings related to the seen world. Our major religions follow the same pattern and, having translated their holy books into the past tense, have fixed histories with fixed positions to defend and attack. We as individuals do exactly the same when we choose to live according to our imagined past histories, seeking to defend and attack those who upset us. Out of a fixed place and a fixed past we will give birth to habits, addictions, disharmony, conflict, stupidity and disease. Healing, vision and understanding are born out of the present tense.

In the dictionary the meaning given for the word 'ancestor' is:

One from whom a person is descended whether on the father's side or the mother's side, at any distance of time, a progenitor, a forefather.

This is a past tense translation that has separated heaven from earth. It assumes that there is no inheritance of anything abstract, or mental before birth. The dictionary was compiled by a people who have forgotten their source, so they designed something that satisfied the needs of those who were in the same mental condition. There are other meanings to consider.

The word 'ancestor' begins with ANC, which is also the beginning of the word ancient. We can try to communicate with the ancestors through the past tense, or through the present tense. Most of us interpret the world through what we think happened to us in our past. These interpretations also include our own feelings and thoughts.

The letter sequence ANC is also related to the word 'ankh', and this symbol or hieroglyph is a sun rising over the horizon or a T shape with a rising sun. The horizontal line is the horizon while the vertical line is its path or its roots through darkness. The ankh symbolically represents one who has the ability to cross the horizon between birth and death, between here and there – one who can pass through the barrier between life and death. The word 'ankh' is hidden in the English language in the word England, Angleland or Anckland. It is a sun crossing from darkness into light. The one who holds this symbol is still in contact with the purpose for which they were sent. It is also related to words like angel, angle and France.

One of the meanings attributed to the word-ending 'ist', as interpreted in the dictionary, is someone who practises a particular belief. This is also a physical interpretation. In the present tense it means that we are being who we are. 'Anc est' then means something like, 'We are the ones who pass between birth and death, the people who have not forgotten the purpose for which we were sent.' Anc also relates to words like angle, angel and France.

'Or' is a word related to the mineral gold. Gold symbolically represents the radiation of the sun. Ancestor is one who can pass through the horizon between here and there. The true purpose of who and what we are is to shine like the sun. Who is this one who passes between the gates on the horizon, whose destiny is to remember to *radiate* in return?

Druids use triads to explain the basic principles of life. Life is translated into movement through the creation of a future, present and past tense, or night and day with the sun in-between. Night and day are dependent upon where the sun is in the sky. Future and past are dependent on where now is. Now is the reality, now is a sun; the future and past do not really exist. The present tense cannot be seen from outside of itself and the only evidence for its existence is to see where it has just been, to see its radiation trail, to see it radiate. The reflection in the mirror is not real, it is an illusion just like the past and future. There is an invisible wall built between now and the past and future, between the unseen and seen.

We work with the illusion to find the reality. We could say that we study the reflection to find the reality of who we are. We study radiation to find out who our ancestors are.

All hieroglyphs can be read in a triadic format, in the centre of the word is the now of the word, at the beginning is the future and at the end is the past. The beginning of the word represents the seed, containing the future potential of the word; in the centre is the purpose of its existence, that which gives it life. The end of the word is its past or the completion of the task, its fruition. Each word is like an agricultural year; each word is like a day and a night. Words are just as alive as our children are. Our words are like ships that set sail out of the harbour of our mouths in the same way that the Ancient Egyptian Sun Barque carried the sun across the skies from here to there. A word in the present tense is alive with the purpose of its being; a word in the past that has lost its connection to its purpose is slowly dying as it substitutes external goals to replace the love it has lost sight of.

The purpose and meaning of life is always with the present tense and the hieroglyph. A triad for language would consist of the hieroglyphic hidden meaning, the life and purpose of the word. The symbolic meaning is the interpretation of source into form. And finally the literal meaning of word, which either kills or resurrects the message.

Another triad is 'I am', my personality and my body. 'I am' is unseen and exists in the present; it is born out of and dies into the present. 'I am' is incarnated many times, and is the seed of causes in our life. We were and are Egypt, Greece and Rome etc. Our immortal self is our ancestor and this self of everyone else is also our ancestor.

Sleep

Life provides plenty of opportunities to experience crossing between life and death, between here and there, but the most obvious one is sleep or rest, which everyone has an experience of. Sleep and rest are necessary to life. At night we go through a process of renewal through which every cell in the body is recycled or revitalised. We have our feelings, thoughts and the link to our purpose renewed so that when we rise in the morning we are ready to begin again. In order to sleep we have to enter the sacred place or present tense, we have to give up our daytime concerns and become nobody or nothing. We have to learn to give up our false sense of importance to sleep well, to let go of our leaves (beliefs). However, if we cannot give up who we think we are then we will find it difficult to sleep. Sleeping pills can alleviate the problem of being self-centred by inducing sleep. We can then sleep, but we become unconscious of now. This is how some of us sleep, we sleep and live unconsciously. We are not aware of one half of life.

The process of sleep involves getting prepared for bed. This involves completing everything we began in the day, accepting those things we have not completed and postponing them until tomorrow. We are reducing ourselves and everything we have learned into a small space ready to travel home to meet the source of our existence. Sleep is a process of making ourselves into a seed and getting into a bed, wrapping ourselves with blankets to maintain our body heat, which will drop in temperature the more removed we become from our material existence. This is the same process as the Ancient Egyptians went through when wrapping a body in material, calling it a mummy and preparing it for entrance into the sacred space or present tense. The seed is then put into a tomb, womb, or bed. According to the Bible, Jesus was put into a cave (chrysalis) and in the morning the stone (blanket) was rolled away and he was resurrected. We then arise from our beds, open the front door and go to work. Chambered mounds are like caves/wombs/tombs/spaces etc. These seeds are compacted genetic codes and plans for future growth and development. The stars at night are the seeds of the universe; they are the larger relatives of the seeds in the earth and the thoughts in our heads.

At night we become nothing, packing everything into a small space we leave on a journey back to where we came from. In our pre-natal formation in the womb we began as small suns or small sparks of light. A child is created in the womb from nothing and we return to that time-machine space every night and recapitulate our own birth, renewing our relationship with our purpose by returning to that which caused our material bodies or our universe. Stars and black holes are like diversity and unity, light radiation and seed making. At night we return from diversity to unity. In birth the fertilised egg follows the same path as the birth of the universe, from electrons to atoms to molecules, from mineral to vegetable and animal kingdoms, they come together to form a body or universe. In becoming nothing we gain access to everything and everything is our ancestor, our material bodies, feelings and thoughts need the elements of fire, water, earth, air and ether to manifest the purpose. We are the manifestation of everything in the universe. We are everything and nothing; there is nothing here that is not elsewhere. We are the stars and also the black holes, we are the expansion and contraction of life, birthing out and returning back to now.

At night we travel through levels of sleep from less deep to more deep, through dreams, which are just over the borderline between sleep and awake. We travel to deeper sleep back through elemental worlds, back through worlds where feelings and thoughts live, back to where thinking is so abstract it is no longer connected with images and words. We return to the present tense, the whole (holy) place of the mysteries. Our material body is revitalised, unnecessary substances are removed and cells are re-lit. Our thoughts and feelings are returned to nothing so that we can begin again with a clean sheet. This is the promise of life if we want to live it. The most important thing to be restored is our original purpose for being, which we may have forgotten. This purpose and the goals that we have chosen to manifest this purpose through are reunited and made ready for a new journey in the morning. There is just as much going on in the night as there is in the day.

In the finite world we need to concentrate on own chosen goals, we need to concentrate on the world of action. In this world we can forget where we came from and why we came, because our first priority is to provide ourselves with somewhere to live, food to eat, experiences to learn from and something to become. We work up from the seed to unpack ourselves into something good, through developing our consciousness and becoming an understanding human being.

At night we return from the world of action, at night time we can see the stars, we can see infinity, we can view an expanded reflection of our own minds, see the stars as seeds, as thoughts, as the external vision of our own minds and bodies. Seeds are possibilities for expansion and shine with the same contained power from which they are created. The universe can be packed into a small space and still have the same power as the whole. At sleep we become time travellers through the infinite space of the stars linked to the internal working of our own minds, which is just another mind of another universe. This world is largely unknown and the pioneers are few. The mind related to the stars is a new frontier and will be for many years to come. It will be studied hand in hand with the stars and with their relationship of how the universe began. We are all looking for the sacred place. How do we gain entrance into this place? What do we have to do to enter change itself?

Stone circles

Stone circles, mounds and pyramids are reflections of heaven on earth. They are not just concerned with the stars and the planets, but also with the whole of life and how it works.

Ancient people did not have microscopes or sophisticated machinery as an aid to study, they did not need them. What they did have is what they could see with their unaided eyes. The sky at night is already an enlarged version of what exists elsewhere, it is already magnified and they were well aware of the link between the mind and the stars. They learned to see in a different way and used language differently to us. The study or use of stone circles is intimately linked with the study of everything else, and these monuments will not be seen for what they are without a development of the mind everywhere else.

Ancient people saw life as a whole (holy) and did not separate life out into different subjects. Life and death were not separated either. The idea of religion is a recent invention, which we have projected onto previous cultures we do not understand. They understood the concept that what is here is also elsewhere or what is not here is nowhere, and they built their buildings to reflect this knowledge. Physics today is no more advanced than astrology used to be, they are two different languages from different cultures. They were scientists of the whole of life and not just a part of it and their use of hieroglyphs and symbols existed in the present tense, there were no word endings or beginnings, full stops or commas, just a continuous line of images just like electrons are in continuous motion. The intrinsic property of language is movement, and it is difficult for us to understand a written language that has more in common with the language of quantum physics than that of spoken language.

'I am teaching' as opposed to 'I am a teacher'. 'I am leading' as opposed to 'I am a leader'. We will not be able to see or understand the signs and symbols of life without seeing and understanding ourselves at the same time. Mysteries are only secrets because we have chosen not to see them, and secrets are not hidden from us because we choose to be blind to them. This is related to the idea that conscious development within ourselves will enable us to see our own secrets and the mysteries within ourselves. Certain ancient people knew that we would forget these things as soon as we were born. As the brain became more crystallised we became more past tense orientated and forgot. To remind us of who we are they left a few things behind, they left behind monuments to how life works, for instance the Great Pyramid at Giza is primarily a very large womb explaining the mysteries of birth and death, the same is true of Stonehenge as well. We have projected our thought patterns onto other cultures because we are blind to their way of thinking. If we do not know who we are then it is not possible to know who others are. We can project our thoughts on to them and create the illusion that we understand them. An orthodox education can impart the appearance of intelligence, but understanding can only come through a relationship with the present tense.

When Druids use the words sun, moon or planets, or Gods and Goddesses we do not just mean them literally, we do not imagine them to be in one place only and in one position only. Things in fixed positions are usually stuck in past tense. There are countless numbers of suns, moons and stars of all sizes, from the enormous to no size at all. So how did the ancients look at the seen world with the naked eye and relate it to life on earth?

A moon reflects the light of the unseen sun onto the earth during a period we call darkness. A moon has no light of its own, it reflects the sunlight and expresses it according to its character. A moon is in between the light source and the earth, in the same way a symbol reflects the meaning of something abstract into something seen. It is an eye and as such it is a doorway between two worlds, the ancestors and us. We cannot look directly at the sun, but we can look at the light indirectly through the moon. If we saw the light directly it may be too bright and we may not like that which we see in that light. We then have some choices to make: accept and take responsibility for that which we see (rare), blame someone else for it (personally or nationally), have a mental breakdown or develop a mental blindness to that which we do not want to see. By considering ourselves as part of the cosmology of becoming, we understand how matter and spirit are conjoined.

The lower womb

The lower womb gives birth to new universes or children. If we can imagine our body as the earth, the moon as our head and the sun as the unseen source, then in the same way the egg in the womb is also a moon reflecting the unseen sunlight (individuality of the child) waiting for a sperm to waken up the egg or sleeping beauty. An egg in the womb is the same as a moon in the night sky, both being influenced by the same lunar and planetary cycles. A cell has a small solar system within it, the moon is the cell nucleus and the cell membrane (memory brain) is the Saturnian edge of the seen solar system, in between Saturn and the moon, the circumference and the centre are the remaining five planets, all of them contributing to the function of the whole (holy) cell.

The upper womb

The upper womb gives birth to words as children. The formation of children in pregnancy is also the way the mind gives birth to a word. The pineal gland roughly in the centre of the brain is the moon responding in the same way to the cycles of light as the egg in the womb. The pineal gland reflects the unseen sun (self of the person) into the earth or body, called in more religious circles the upper room or womb, the northern mountain, the hill of Golgotha. It has a direct relationship with the crown worn by royalty, which was originally a statement that they were representatives of the pole star on earth. The crown itself represents the pole star constellations. Saturn at the edge of the seen solar system is that which is furthest away from the light, the skin is ruled by Saturn. The pineal gland representing the moon reflects the unseen light into the physical body or earth (see *Meditations 1 and 2 below*). We are born through a prism from the world of white into the world of colour and we disappear from the world of colour back into a world of white. The spinal column (pineal column) is represented in many cultures as a sacred river, the Ganges, the Nile. Consider the letter P as the upper womb on a spinal column, lower case b as the lower womb on a spinal column and capital B as both together.

Light and dark

Light and dark are illusions because there is only the present tense. Where the light has just been or where it has not yet arrived does not exist. We live in what we would call the daytime, working in the past tense looking for the light of the present tense in the darkness. Ancient people would have described living in the daytime world as living in darkness. In Ancient Egypt the underworld was called Amenta or in English the mental world, the world we cannot see. Their God of writing, or more precisely thinking, is called Thoth or in English *thought*. We live in the darkness in a mental world of past tense illusion trying to find the present tense or Egyptian Goddess Isis (virgin space) or what IS is.

Stone circles, or other so-called religious spaces, have an informing centre and an edge that reflects the Saturnian cycle and in between representations of planets and elements.

A stone circle could be related to a cell structure, a womb, a brain and many other contexts. Stone is used because it is the lowest and most solid of materials and the mineral kingdom is the best conductor of light, the highest works through the lowest. The lower the pupil, the higher the teacher. The spinal column is a mineral. Consciousness develops its way up through the mineral, vegetable, animal and human kingdoms until there is no difference between the teacher and the pupil. The centre and the edge become unified. The same idea relates to how the wealthy relate to the poor, the highest works through the lowest. In the end there must be a unity between the wealthy and poor, an equality of honour.

Triads

Symbolic buildings communicate how the world of life and death work, not just on a physical level, but on an emotional and mental level as well. To change something all three levels must be included. Temples, like wombs, have two entrances or exits, one for the physical to enter and one for the light to enter. Stonehenge, the Great Pyramid and the womb have two entrances one for the people and one for the light, the real invisible seed of causes. There are always three points to every creation. The man provides a sperm, the woman provides an egg; the unseen individuality of the child brings them together. A marriage must have three points; it is not a marriage if it only includes a man and a woman. They are married to a purpose, which brought them together. This is the same as introducing the present between past and future without which there is no life or movement in the relationship.

Altars

The moon or symbol translates source into form. The moon in the circle is an altar, because it is the place of alteration or transformation. This ever-moving place called now is a time machine, which we can disappear into, and then reappear.

Altars, just like moons, exist everywhere but are only accessible through the present tense, called in religious language the sacred place. Altars exist in churches as symbols of redemption. Looking eastwards towards the altar we would have seen a screen protecting the present tense from those who live in the past. In the centre of the screen is a birthing stool, representing change. Behind the screen sits the choir representing angels (anckels) and finally the altar with resurrection symbols on it; resurrection can only come through the present tense (woman). Some of these symbols have mostly disappeared from churches.

Altars also exist in shops, which have counters with tills on them representing the moon. We sacrifice our money (mooney) into them, and the product of our desire is resurrected in its place heralding good times to come, for at least two weeks anyway. Shopping is a fertility rite, which we have inherited and interpreted into the past tense. We use many past tense activities to remind us of what it feels like to be alive. We have lost contact with the radiation and health which was once ours, so now we seek external material in the form of drugs, sugar, TV etc to assist us in this pretence. The ability to allow oneself to be changed is potency; we are impotent if we cannot enter the present tense. We are very clever at pretending to be able to heal, think and act like individuals. Only the present tense can heal, think, change, and transform and support our individuality.

The unseen suns are our ancestors and we can only communicate with them through the present tense, otherwise it will be a dead history and no amount of modern multimedia interpretation can make it look otherwise.

Group formation

We can find a way back and communicate with the ancestors again and restore the magic that was once ours, enabling us to meet the need in the present. We can set up groups to function after the pattern of a womb, a mind, a cell, or a solar system. A group that wants to communicate with the ancestors needs to have a fertilisation point; the moon is a fertilisation point for light to be transmitted to the earth, the egg in the womb is a fertilisation point to begin the formation of a body to facilitate action in a new world. The pupil in the centre of the eye acts as an impregnation point for the light. The pineal gland operates as a fertilisation point for the brain. All of these points are fertilised from outside of their space, the information that impregnates them comes from another unseen world. The present tense or now is an egg in-between the future and the past, it is also fertilised by the light from somewhere else. This process, of how life propagates itself and how thoughts arrive in our heads from apparently nowhere, is the basis of seeing and understanding. It is how potential becomes an action. Together, we can set up groups to function as a mirror to the universe.

The physical leader of the group must be chosen and not inherited, chosen equals choice, inherited leadership has no choice. Inheritance is an attempt to perpetuate the past, whereas choice provides the opportunity for change to happen. There is no democracy in a system dependent upon inheritance to control the present. In another context there is no democracy in the dictionary if its inheritance is an attempt to freeze the past at a particular point in history.

Although there are millions of sperm heading towards the egg there is only one chosen, there is only one verb, the verb 'to be being' and that verb is the ancestor of language just as the light within everyone is an extension of the one light (verb). The group must choose to be unified through one leader. The body and personality of each individual must also have one leader within themselves. The chosen leader needs to be acceptable to the unseen sun of the group, which carries the purpose and meaning of that group, and the members who do the choosing. In this kind of endeavour the unseen ones have the capacity to pull towards or reject people into or away from the group even against their conscious will. This also applies to pregnancy. The chosen group leader is now linked with the purpose of the unseen ones, or consciousness of the group. This consciousness includes other members both present and long since dead. All can be present at meetings. Most of these patterns also apply to getting pregnant or to receiving an inspired thought in our minds from an unseen source. There are two apparent choices, the unseen spirit of the child chooses its parents and the parents choose to facilitate this choice. The same relationship exists between I am, me and my body, I am chooses the body and personality, the body and personality facilitate I am.

If we want to form a circle or a circle of spinal columns (stones), we need the following requirements:

(a) We need to approach our circle in the atmosphere in which we want it to be held. Avoid inappropriate contacts before we meet; start getting ourselves into the right frame of mind before it is due to begin.

(b) The circle leader must have absolute authority. There can only be one informing centre for the group. Each individual has their own informing centre, which they are responsible for. The leader teaches the group, the group teaches the teacher.

(c) Cultivate the right attitude to one another. Remove all disruptive people who will bring inharmonious elements to the circle, disturbing conditions or hampering any serious work.

(d) Procedure: Opening; leader's instructions, work for the meeting, reports; closing. This follows the pattern of morning, noon and evening. Each meeting should be timed to run for the estimated period decided upon. It should not be left to fade out.

(e) Avoid interruptions.

A basic meditation exercise to assist communication with the ancestors, immortals or our own internal light is as follows.

Meditation 1

Sit upright in a chair and relax, bring up to date all the daily issues not yet resolved, or leave them alone for a while. Forget who you think you are, forget all reasons why you are meditating at all.

Balance your breath so it is equal in and out. Make the breath longer than your usual breath.

Concentrate your awareness in the centre of the forehead, be conscious from that point, view the stream of your feelings and thoughts from a higher place.

Create with your imagination a circle of light travelling in an anti-clockwise direction around yourself or around the group, following the apparent path of the sun.

Illuminate your spinal column from the base up into the head around and connect it to the centre in your forehead. Your spinal column radiates light out in all directions.

If you lose any of these exercises, just return back to the relaxation and begin again, do not lose focus and fall into a daydream state or allow daily thoughts to lead you off in to a state of unconsciousness.

Meditation 2

Imagine a sphere (fertilisation point) of shining light higher up and in the centre of the circle.

On the in breath imagine drawing a shaft of light from this sphere towards your forehead and then down your spinal column to the base. On the out breath radiate light out in all directions from the spinal column into a sphere of light surrounding the whole group.

In this exercise the group acts as the generator of light, by creating a sphere. The sphere in the centre acts like an aerial for incoming information from another level of being. This aerial is a moon sending shafts of light to the members that make up the body of the group. Each member then responds by radiating this light out from the spinal column into a sphere surrounding the whole group. This group organism has a receiving and returning action. It breathes in and out; it is organic and expresses the same aliveness as anything else does as long as it fulfils the purpose of its creation.

The pituitary gland has a direct relationship with the pineal gland, allowing the light of the visible sun to awaken the pineal gland through the physical eyes. The physical eyes see the past. The pituitary gland can also allow the light of invisible suns to awaken the pineal gland to its longer-than-one-life memory. It can facilitate seeing in the present through the forehead. White light dies into a prism and appears in colour on the other side, an idea is born. Meditation creates a state of nothingness. The ancestors cannot communicate if we are obsessed by who we think we are, they need us to create a meeting place, a mind between the abstract (ab-star-ct) and the physical. We could allow the son of Ceridwen, Avaag ddu, to be changed from the ugly deformed one into Taliesin of the radiant brow. In the Welsh myth, Afagddu ap Ceridwen was born so ugly that his mother brewed in her cauldron a draught of wisdom that would compensate him: but the one who benefitted from the brew was Gwion, whose rebirth as the child Taliesin, enabled his omniscience.

> A basic group circle is an instrument that can be used to achieve almost any desired end, if we know how to achieve it. As a field of scientific research it has not been thoroughly explored. When spiritual science has been as efficiently and properly investigated as any other science, it will take the lead of all the sciences. When we form a group or circle, we need to make up our minds between ourselves as to what we want to achieve; then experiment to see if we can get it. When the pupil is ready the master will appear.
>
> (From *Home Circles* by Dr Thomas Maughan)

When an idea's time has come the people will see the need. When we ask a question the answer will also appear. Create the conditions and we will get the results. When we are ready the ancestors will answer the call.

The Heart of the Land:
The Druidic Connection

By Penny Billington

Although the connection is technically immeasurable, we humans instinctively feel that we have a bond with the earth that cries for recognition. A reaction against a logical, reductionist view of the world is fast gaining hold among people wishing to reclaim a relationship with nature. We recognise its necessity for our physical, mental, emotional and spiritual health – and this has resulted in a massive rise in interest in earth-based religions.

But the need to acknowledge a relationship with nature is not limited to those with an interest in spiritual matters. In mainstream society it is fed through our abiding interest in gardening/nature programmes, window boxes and herb growing – even from the most determinedly urban of us. And the more overt expression of an inner urge to be in nature has now passed into cultural respectability – annual pilgrimages to open air festivals such as Glastonbury or gatherings to celebrate the winter and summer solstices at Stonehenge.

The fact that these huge gatherings are in landscapes resonant with myth and ancestral connotations is no accident. For behind, and informing, the urge to be in nature is a yearning which, acknowledged or not, is spiritual. It is to connection: a basic beyond-rational understanding that we are not separate, as modern life insists, but are all linked in an intricate web of life. Acknowledging this frees us from the lie that the everyday world insists on; that we are isolate and our only solace is to grope for a human contact doomed to be imperfect. We feel intuitively that we might have the potential to connect to all living beings on the planet; and we know from our dreams and from periods of intense joy and intense trauma, that we are capable of experiencing more than one kind of reality. Extreme experiences take us beyond time and space as we usually relate to it, showing that other ways of relating are possible. The world is not as we have always imagined. It is a living and wise entity, and it has a beating and resonant heart.

To access earth wisdom we start not by journeying to mysterious landscapes, but through exploring nature in our locality, where in a long gone and simpler world the buzzing of the bees sang the story of the honey that would be eaten on homemade bread. Romantic? Yes, but also true, for those songs are still sung today, throughout the natural world. We simply need to explore, both in the landscape and in our private territory of mind and imagination.

As an antidote to the orderly process of reading, imagine yourself for a moment on a hill at sunset, with the quiet buzzing of the insects invisible in the soft light. From your vantage point you look over the dark lake to the west, where the molten streaks of light reflect in a shimmering water-path leading to you, and with the quiet stars appearing in the deep blue overhead. This momentary turning of our attention to the world of nature, even in the imaginal realm, can prompt a surprising sense of relaxation that slows our breathing and our over-busy brains.

Feeling a connection intuitively, it is reassuring to find that science backs up these instincts. Scientists have long known that, like the simplest sea-organisms responding to moon and tide, humans are keyed into the rhythms of the world in which we live. Remove us from all external stimuli and substitute artificial rhythms – 23 or 25 hour days – and we will not adapt to them; our physical, mental and emotional health will suffer drastically. Just as the simplest orders of the natural kingdom respond to tide and temperature, so our core selves remain firmly wedded to the natural world of which we are a part. And, if we accept the harmony of nature, then, even in spite of our society's despoliation of the natural world, we are an essential part, with a right to our place. What we do with that place is our very pressing responsibility, but we should not think of ourselves as stewards in a way that elevates us. We co-exist; we fit in, as does every other species. The only difference is that we have the ability to regulate our effects on the world, and so it is our moral duty to do so.

These rhythmic associations are the reality by which we can measure our lives. We can liken childhood, youth, maturity and old age to spring, summer, autumn and winter; we picture spring as a garlanded youth, and death as the ancient skeletal man with the scythe of the harvest, as previous generations receding back into ancient times have done. Like the flora and fauna of the rest of the natural world, we grow, seed and die, and our bodies enrich the soil.

At a time when society seems fragmented and fragile, offering little stability of family, job or accommodation, it is no wonder that dirt- forest- and eco-therapy, forest schools, therapeutic gardening and Green Care/exercise are all becoming valued therapies. This is not only in a remedial way for specific problems, but as mainstream injections into our educational system. It is our recognition that we need to counteract the malaise current in society – the divorce from nature that Western civilisation, aided by the growth of modern technologies, has been assiduously courting for decades. Populist attempts at antidotes come continuously from programmes that stream into our homes. As well as the practical advice and hands-on engagement with the reality of the food chain, there is a prolifer-ation of archaeological/historical programmes addressing the spiritual symbolism and implications of our ancient landscapes.

Communicating with the ancestral heart serves to redress the balance within, and return us to a life more rooted in reality. For a conscious relationship with nature nourishes our spirit, and simultaneously has two main effects. The first, as we stand watching that magnificent sunset, is to bring back to our overloaded brains a sense of perspective. By concentrating on something larger than and outside our petty concerns, we begin to let go, to allow, to come back to a centred, grounded way of being in the world. The second effect is to simultaneously diminish us by scale – how important are we in the greater scheme of things? – and also to enlarge us; for we, by our awareness, are an essential part of the moment, the magnificent spectacle of the sun's descent. We have a right to be here, and we are serving the scene by witnessing it. We come back down the hill refreshed, and a little more in touch, a little saner, perhaps, than when we went up it.

From our earliest mythological tales to the present day, withdrawing to the natural world has been a cure for extreme trauma. As animals go to hide when sick, so do we. It has always been so. Our present-day Vietnam war veterans who took to the wilderness for healing are in a long tradition. I wonder if this explains the urge to escape to the countryside after the First World War, when swathes of the population took to the land for holidays, coining the phrase 'I'm happy when I'm hiking'? Their instinct to 'claim' the land, placing railway carriages and caravans in small plots, alarmed the authorities to the extent that prompted the Town and Country Planning Acts. And if we look to the ancient past for eco-therapy, we can find a noble precedent in British mythology, for 'back to the land' has been efficacious as a cure since the time of King Arthur's advisor, Merlin. After the battle of Arfderydd, where he witnessed the slaughter of his relatives, he was inconsolable and ran mad in the Caledonian Forest, living as a wild man, until the time came for him to reintegrate to society. So today, nature contact, the beating heart of the natural world, is still there on the outskirts of every town, in the huge parks of our cities, to help alleviate and heal the everyday stresses of our lives.

The search for the ancestral heart in nature is, in part, a romantic notion, born of our removal from the realities of regular wetting, scratching and stinging that being in the wild occasions. When we lived close to the soil, our literature shows that wild nature was feared – think of the terrifying wood in *A Midsummer Night's Dream*. After the Industrial Revolution and the migration to urban life, nature began to be seen through rose-coloured spectacles. Poets wrote of Arcadian times that had gone: and today, isolated by cars and central heating, we have that as an ideal – until the car breaks down in the wilds as darkness begins to fall, when our view of nature alters radically and becomes immediately more real. Connection to nature means a connection to reality.

Interestingly, the Classical writers expressed the same dichotomy in their commentaries on the ancient Druids. Like nature itself, they were perceived both as 'red in tooth and claw' – a murderous priesthood – and harmonious and gentle, the teachers of natural lore, poetry and the spiritual arts. Such reportage has to do with propaganda, spin and the distance between written events and actual evidence – although it is not our job to try to whitewash our spiritual forebears, whose moral and ethical code was doubtless appropriate to the time, circumstances and their understanding of the world. Our obligation is simply to take what is creative and regenerating from the old, to craft a spirituality that is relevant, with a morality and ethics that suits the dictates of our own consciences and is acceptable to the wider society in which we live.

For reading between the contradictory reports over hundreds of years of the extremes of blood-soaked altars and of philosophers steeped in knowledge of the natural sciences, we find many hints of a settled spiritual approach to a life rooted in the soil. From these, we can begin to hone a spirituality both rooted in the land and relevant to the future. Druids are beguiling to our modern sensibilities: they beckon from the forest, standing on the cusp of myth and history. In search of the ancestral heart, the connection both to our forebears and to the land, they are wonderful guides. They feed our sense of romance while encouraging us to make a real grass-roots connection; not through books or spells or the imaginal realm – although all of these might be useful to us – but first and foremost by getting out into the wild places and the forests, the parks and gardens. No matter how restricted our mobility, nature is just outside our window.

So we turn to the Druids; a traditional land-based priesthood enshrined in history and legend. But, when dealing with heart-connection, we must be fluid in our definitions: every person must feel they can expand their understanding of the ancestral heart to fill the perfect space within. So, although the Ancient Druids had their base in Britain, there is nothing exclusive to any one country about Druidry. From the few Roman and Greek sources we learn something especially relevant to our restless society – that students came from many countries to learn from the Druids, the judges, arbiters, holders of authority and the laws. So we can safely assume that they would return to incorporate that learning into the existing wisdom of their tribes. Here we have historical precedent that those lessons are of value anywhere. They can be transplanted across the globe to help fashion a relevant, nature-based practice on whatever terrain we find ourselves. And it seems obvious that, as our bodies still tick to the same cosmic clock that our forebears were governed by, their wisdom will still be relevant in our task of fashioning a coherent understanding of our myriad relationships, cosmic, (super)natural and human: a spiritual approach to life in the 21st century.

To most people, the word 'Druid' evokes an image of a bearded man in a white robe. That image comes largely from charming 18th century pictures. Yet the Romans mentioned Druidesses, and a look at tribal societies will give us a view of their appearance and practice that is likely to be far more realistic.

And although Druidry had most definitely reached a cultural

full flowering around the time of the Roman Invasion, those Iron Age priests are not the only ones entitled to the name; that again, like a crude nationalistic approach, would be far too limiting. For those Druids that Julius Caesar et al. wrote about undoubtedly drew on earlier wisdom from the Neolithic and the Bronze Age. These predecessors can be considered proto-Druids; those who have been the indigenous priests of the land, who have observed the relationship between people and earth since the beginning of time and whose wisdom undoubtedly filtered down to successive generations. Archaeological thinking is now far more in favour of this idea of gradual cultural changes than of a fracturing of existing tradition by each succeeding wave of aggressive incomers.

This wisdom, gleaned from a million hints in landscape, a thousand sunsets and dreaming full moons, has no dogma. The Druids are an ideal source of inspiration, for they feed our yearning and give us pointers, yet allow space for our own imaginative connections. From the finite primary source material we can know so much, but never any more. It is as if, on the very edge of the known, recorded world, we have glimpses through the mists of time – and Druids famously could control the mists – offering us a system of understanding. The mystery surrounding the Druids reflects the mystery that is the basis of all religious urgings; it is beyond understanding.

Try to gain certainty – usually through logical analysis – and we will lose the mystery, the magic. Literal thinking has no place here; we must engage fully with the concept of different, but equally valid realities. In spirituality, the imaginal, inner world is afforded equal weight with that of the five senses. So no one will ever dig up the actual Holy Grail – or its ancestral prototype, the Welsh cauldron of Annwn; but we can become aware of its presence and experience its influence within us. The contact can only exist in intangible realms and deep, imaginal spaces that are never far away, and are easily accessible through relaxation and the imagination.

But even this inner contact is not necessary to absorb the lessons and blessings of the natural world. Just walk in the country until your feet find their natural pace and rhythm, moving automatically, and you are not conscious of having a thought in your head. Then sit quietly and listen to birdsong until it is time to return. You will have been further than just a couple of miles; deeper into yourself and your relationship with nature, without the pesky logical brain butting in and trying to take charge, as usual. You will feel energised, yet calm: refreshed. In some way, you will have learnt something from your native soil, wherever you live in the world and whatever the terrain. You will have deepened your relationship with it, and had the experience of 'nature as teacher' – and it was so simple. The place to connect to the ancestral heart is in our locality; the time is now.

Let us turn now to what has been written about the Druids, in the commentaries of their chroniclers and their enemies. We learn that they were a priesthood who travelled; they were learned and were respected by Greek men of letters. They could adjudicate, arbitrate and cite genealogies back through many generations to maintain tribal stability. They believed in the eternity of the soul, and in reincarnation. They understood the mysteries of the natural world, the turning mysteries of the planets and they conducted ritual in forest settings – and from the early Brythonic and Goidelic languages, the word 'Druid' is connected to 'oak tree', 'knowledge', and to the Greek 'sorcerer' and 'seer'. Druidesses, particularly, are documented as having the gift of prophecy; and we have instructions on how the Druids gathered healing plants in a ritual fashion. There were three distinctions; firstly, the bards, who excelled both at praise songs and excoriating criticisms; who could walk between warring armies and the fighting would stop. The Euates, now commonly called Ovates, attempted to explain the high mysteries of nature;

and the Druids were inspired philosophers, spiritual seekers and with a position of responsibility in the community. Their exemption from taxation is a bittersweet consideration for most modern Druids.

They were persecuted, one suspects, not for their religious learning – the Romans had a good track record of incorporating local deities and substituting them into their pantheons of Gods, as in 'Sulis Minerva' the Goddess of the hot springs of Bath – but for the danger the Druids posed in giving coherence to the autonomous tribal system. Druids would travel between the tribes, dispensing judgements and justice, and were as respected as kings. And, through prodigious feats of memory, they held the genealogies of the kings, a vital role in a system of autonomous kingdoms where matriarchal lineage, the wide habit of fosterage, and partible inheritance, resulted in a complex system of ties and obligations hard to imagine from our isolated system of patriarchy, the nuclear family and primogeniture.

Their second point of power was in their huge repository of teaching stories and histories, all disseminated orally, for it was forbidden to write them down. But Julius Caesar did report that Druids knew the mysteries of the natural world and the movements of the heavenly bodies. Learning about, and gaining understanding of, the rhythms of the natural world is key to modern Druids too. We take on board the challenge to feel the pulse of life, to go with the flow in a way that promotes the likelihood of maximising the good times and minimising the bad. By going to the forest, we try to slow down to the pulse of the earth, to attune. We have several ancient instructions for magical harvesting and working with herbs, and modern Druids take health and natural healing very seriously. We know that our ancient forebears were of service to their societies and were respected for their gifts; and as well as gaining a personal spiritual benefit, we try to live up to that wider example in our own lives.

In crafting our own path, we look next at the physical evidence on the landscape.

We've noted that the recognised time of the Druids is much later than the monuments we will find, yet the builders and celebrants within them can be regarded as proto-Druids: indigenous priests of the land. What matters is the celebration of the connection to the natural world, as a way of informing a way of life and understanding of the esoteric aspects of the universe. In engaging with the ancestral heart, we find the secrets of the landscape are hidden in full view of all. In antiquity, the land was, at various stages, modified by huge workforces; the legacy from our forebears. Wherever we look in Britain we find standing stones, henges, round barrows, singly and in cemeteries, long barrows, cursus, ancient track-ways and chalk carvings.

These are all quiet yet potent presences, to speak of the work and long-disappeared beliefs of our ancestors of blood and spirit. They tell us that those long gone understood the mysteries of the heavens, just as Julius Caesar reported, and that they marked the seasons of the sun in stone. They tell us that circles, ellipses and trackways were sacred to them, and through the archaeology of the cultural changes in death rites we can see their ideas change and develop, into an age of status and individuality that we can recognise and identify with in our own times.

Visiting sacred complexes inspires us to speculate on the lives of their makers. Many incorporate cemetery mounds, bringing home to us the reality of our forebears literally as part of the earth that we walk on – the large harvest mounds near our henges pique our curiosity as to just what they meant to a society long gone.

In the Vale of the White Horse, in Oxfordshire, one can easily walk from the Neolithic long barrow of Wayland's Smithy to the White Horse, a strange dragon-like hill figure seemingly stencilled on the chalk through the greensward, and galloping across the hills. In doing so we are traversing a two thousand year span of physical evidence of belief and practice; we are time travelling back five thousand years to the time of the barrow's construction by men with antler picks. We can explore the physical landscape, wherever we are in the world, and then we can look at ancient Celtic place names all over Europe – a huge study in itself and including places including the word 'Nemeton' – Celtic for sacred grove. Such hints are never far away.

Considering archaeologists' conclusions about society contemporary with the Druids we may find surprising similarities with our own. Probably the majority of us live in a multi-cultural environment whose difference and diversity is immensely enriching; yet we hold largely to our own ancestral cultural habits, as indoctrinated by our family groups and in the habits of childhood. If we think of our extended family as our tribe, the similarities become more apparent. The society influenced by the Druids was intensely individualistic, like ours. It loved bling – one of the most startling variations in burial practice was the flamboyant and costly chariot burial, confined to the East Riding of Yorkshire. They loved heroism and the tales tell us that they valued personal honour above winning. There was no concept of nationalism, but many tribal ties were spread across a wide area – for example, the Parisii tribe, with branches in both Britain and Gaul. It is no wonder that Celtic society was ultimately dominated by the military tactics of the Romans.

Yet, despite variations of tribal practice, in Britain and Europe there is a continuous strand of belief in an afterlife and in Gods who inhabit a world that is certainly accessible from ours. There is liminal time when this is most likely – dusk, dawn, midday and midnight, and the deeply unsettling mist and fog. There is liminal space, neither one thing nor the other, where we can touch other realms – the worlds of the living and the dead, of humankind and the Gods. The top of a mountain, the bowels of a cave, the seashore, the meeting place between cultivated land and wild – all are portal places and enshrined as such in our most ancient tales.

We know that in lakes, fast-flowing rivers and marshland, our ancestors made votive offerings; they gave gifts from this world to the realm of the Gods through the portal of deep water. The objects found, rusted, bent and twisted, need an archaeologist's eye to tell us that these were frequently of immense personal and tribal status: personal and ritual artifacts and jewellery, chains, shields and swords, objects so costly that their possession must have conferred status on a whole tribe. The ritual act of relinquishing them to the Otherworld must have been immensely significant. It is hard to understand this in modern-day context; taking the plasma TV and all our electronic toys and throwing them away, watching them disappear into a sinking marsh, might give us some inkling. And these offerings were deposited in truly huge quantities.

Some objects were deliberately bent to ensure they could never again be used, reminding us of the superstition that iron, weapons and things of the earth are of no use in the Otherworlds: others were brand new and perfect, an offering of what was most precious fresh from the forging, and unsullied by this world.

Returning in imagination to our picture of the sun sinking and the lake shimmering below, we can take a moment to wonder what treasure might lie quiet beneath the water, and for what purpose it was deposited. And that can conjure an image of the stirring of the water, and the magical sword Excalibur slowly rising, a gift from the Otherworlds; one of the many symbols of kingship, and a weapon whose value is only superseded by the scabbard that contains it.

Who knows what deep ancestral memories of votive offerings have ensured the continuance of that legend? What ancient resonances, of gifting and relinquishing, well up when our children throw a coin into a city centre fountain, as if a portal might open and magical wonders emerge from another world. Ancestral remembrance is deep within us, and frequently stirs in its slumber.

The whole widespread practice of votive offering is a lesson to us in reciprocity with nature. In current tribal societies, gift giving at significant times is the tangible expression of gratitude. In the Western world we are rather in the mindset of tit for tat, 'You give me a present, so I give you one.' But this is irrelevant to an expanded worldview. If all our actions tremble a larger web of connection, then every act of awareness, thought and kindness is one of gratitude. Gaining an enlarged sense of life from witnessing the sunset flows through the body and mind, and makes reciprocating part of a natural flow and interaction with the whole of life. It might and should take many forms – from something as simple as scattering nuts and raisins for wildlife or feeding the birds in our garden to the complexities of saving your environment from inappropriate development.

The ancestral heart is found not only through the landscape but also deep within. Caitlín Matthews has made the point that when a living tradition is fractured or broken, it does not die, but sleeps in various ways – in the landscape itself, and as an inheritance of deep inner understanding that can still be accessed. The lessons of Druidry continue to be celebrated and passed on through folklore and myth that reverberate back into the past and deep into our psyche. This is our ancestral store, a precious repository of treasure. If we go to live abroad, it will travel with us, and stay deep within to inform and mediate our actions and reactions as we come to an accommodation with the reality and the myths – the ancestral heart – of our adopted country. Lacking these is a source of our yearning, as if our jigsaw has missing pieces. When we discover them, their wisdom sinks deep within, to colour an internal landscape coherent with that which we can view out of the window; they help to join us up within and without.

For many of our ancestors, worldwide, had a mythopoetic view of the landscape that connected them to the ancestral heart. It is an entirely different way of relating to the topography, and roots us firmly into the places of birth and of living. Mythopoetic thought regards living things as persons, not objects, and relationship is the natural result of that understanding. Reclaiming it as our right can transform our relationships and allow our intuitive understanding to flower into a new and expanded view. If both we, and other species, are all persons, then it is entirely natural to expect to communicate. We do it automatically with our pets, never allowing the brain to put us off with an insistence that the lack of language in that communication makes it invalid. It then becomes a logical progression to communicate with trees, lakes and whole landscapes; to adopt, perhaps, the magical mind-set of the Druids of old.

The oldest myths, folklore and poetry of our islands were written down in the early mediaeval period. But linguists detect vestiges of an old oral tradition, and ways of thinking, acting and expression within the tales that probably place their origins centuries earlier. Within this precious store we find poets who can become other beings and have experience of the elements – who claim kinship with every aspect of the world through relationship. We see princes transformed to animals as retribution and princesses supported by their totems in times of hardship. We find kings who enter liminal space – the wildwood, the high mound, the deep cave – to be transported to Annwn, the deep place of making, or to experience magical wonders, or to see their land transformed. And we find the land of myth enshrined in the names of real locations scattered across Wales. The mythic journeys and places of magical experiences written in the *Mabinogion*, the Mound of Arberth, hill of wonders; Mochdrev (swine's town), Mochnant (swine's brook) and Creuwyryon, where Gwydion made a sty for them – can all be visited.

From the earliest Welsh sources also we find the origins of the body of material known as 'The Matter of Britain'– the tales of King Arthur that speak to our souls. Their power is shown by their enduring appeal and relevance, for they are reworked by every generation. The evolution of Arthur has been adapted to the needs of successive generations, from the times of the mediaeval kings – where a supposed Arthurian connection shored up the validity of their kingship – to modern television re-workings that feed our need for depth of myth in a superficial age.

What makes the Arthurian myth so special is part of the essential mystery of spiritual connection. It satisfies us firstly by being aspirational; the knights live by an idealistic code. Then it is keyed into the world as a magical place and reminds us that we should regard the wonders of the universe with awe. It shows us a society that has coherence. Our blessing, and curse, is that rigid social distinctions have largely broken down. It has left us bewildered, with an overwhelming choice, but has also opened up huge possibilities to move, change and grow; to live in a more fluid and responsive way than ever before. With such freedom, it is important to find and have clarity around our own place in the world, and teaching stories can guide us. Lastly, through reading them we imbibe lessons all unknowing that will lead us to a greater understanding of ourselves.

Going to a Welsh poem – the *Preiddeu Annwn* (The Spoils of Annwn) – of an heroic quest led by Arthur, there is a symbolism that gives life to the legend. Arthur leads a sortie into Annwn, the Otherworld, the deep, bright, non-place of making, to win a cauldron. Being won from the magical place of creation, the cauldron stands for nurture and regeneration; it is another of the fundamental symbols of kingship to our forebears. It is an inner resource to keep us nourished and whole. And it is ever-present through the *Mabinogion* stories in various guises – leather bags, brass cauldrons, the wombs of the matriarchs of the Islands. To later generations, it would become the Holy Grail, the ultimate quest for the Knights of King Arthur. It reminds us of what is possible; that we too can journey to places other than the apparent world, to bring back inner treasures that will regenerate our lives.

Coming at the legends from another angle brings us, of course, back to the land. For which came first, the spiritual chicken or the powerful glamour of the egg? Put simply, we can consider whether the legends placing Arthur in specific locations sacralise the land by association; or whether land regarded as especially sacred in the first place naturally attract legends of importance to it? Both, of course, might be true. Whatever the truth, the myth must conform to the topography: desert myths do not flourish on temperate soil.

From these thoughts, it is a short step to the idea of the narrative spirit of the land – basically, that the terrain inspires a response within us that prompts the right story to be told. The land has its story to tell, and there are certain spots all over the world accepted as powerful, that draw myth as iron filings are drawn to a magnet. The land itself can use us to articulate its story and being in its ambience inspires us to associate it with powerful myth and legend. It is a logical extension of the mythopoetic view of the world. It is an association that can be found wherever in the world we happen to live.

We can look briefly at Glastonbury, a small market town in the South-West of England, as an ideal example of the land bursting to inspire us to tell its story. Part of that is its especial importance to the Arthurian mythos, through mythic association, archaeological inference, synchronicity of place names and the reputed finding and re-interment of Arthur and his queen by the monks six years after the disastrous Abbey fire of 1184. The town is also part of a gigantic landscape zodiac, with Arthur taking the centaur role of Sagittarius. And in our business of making connections, we remember that the zodiac itself can stand for the round table, brought as a wedding gift by Guenevere to Arthur; symbol of the harmony and unity of the land. As above, so below: the landscape zodiac seems to reflect a map of the stars on a colossal scale, formed by landscape features (roads, streams, field boundaries and so on). It was discovered as a result of Katherine Maltwood's work on 'The High History of the Holy Grail' and introduced to the public as *A Guide to Glastonbury's Temple of the Stars* in 1934. The fact that it does not stand up to serious investigation does not diminish its potency as a symbol of the sacred nature of the land to modern questers. Sometimes objective and spiritual reality must be allowed their own separate spaces, and each outlook respected for what it is.

From round table of the stars to heart and grail, the position of Glastonbury, half way along the Michael Line, which runs diagonally across country from coast to coast, has been considered by many occultists and mystical Christians the 'heart centre' of the country, holding the elixir of love and spirituality hidden deep within its landscape configurations.

Arthur, the peripatetic Iron Age Celtic horse soldier, has a strong presence in this location, in both Dark Age and mythic Christian associations. Given his ancient Welsh origins, it is interesting that the Tor and surrounding hills also host Welsh deities – most obviously Gwyn ap Nudd, who lives under Glastonbury Tor, and possibly the mother Goddess Don at nearby Compton Dundon.

This raises an important point: our ancestral land is too resonant to belong exclusively to one mythic strain. The land around Glastonbury is peopled with sacred tracks, waters, hills and trees – oaks and yews, miraculous thorns and the apple orchards that perfume the land. All is burgeoning, expressive; component parts of a landscape story for those who can hear its whispers. The mixing and allowing of spiritual influences makes Glastonbury a place of power especially significant to anyone crafting their own spiritual connections with the ancestral heart.

As we are active in co-creating our lives, we are wise to note that Glastonbury shows by example that she belongs to no one. Spiritual influence will flow and meld, thin and then coalesce, and express itself in a way that will be appropriate for the time. There seems to be a quality in the land that defies ownership by any one group or belief system. Here in the 21st century, Pagan and Christian mythology exist peacefully side by side. The myth of the Welsh Pagan Arthur combines with that of the Christian king with a wealth of imagery to flood the spiritual senses. Under Chalice Hill, the rounded green dome that is dwarfed by the high Tor, the ancient cauldron becomes the buried chalice whose blood colours 'the blood spring' running iron-red through pilgrimage gardens given an international World Peace Garden designation in 2001.

On the outskirts of town we find Pomparles Bridge, its name remembering the last perilous stage of the journey to the holy Celtic Isle of Avalon. Here we find Beckery, dedicated to the Celtic Goddess Bride who is also St Bridget of the Abbey. Here there is a tradition of an old Druid college, and that local Druids welcomed the earliest Christians, recognising that the spiritual flame is rekindled, expressing itself appropriately in each age of men; and here the Pagan revival flourishes in its turn. The land welcomes and allows all who come to make their own connections, and accepts those who come with the right spirit.

In land widely recognised as 'sacred' the message is overt; but we must remember that every land can be as welcoming, and has equal potential. Maybe it is our witnessing and venerating the hill, the well, the mound, and the cave over generations that builds up the sacral silt, so that its atmosphere can be felt by the pilgrim. If so, the challenge becomes whether we can then activate our own lands by our awareness of their essential sacred nature, and how long it will take the land to respond, so that action prompts reaction in an enriching flow of awareness and appreciation. All we need to do to start the process is to be still and listen; to communicate with the spirits of the non-human persons (Harvey 2005) who co-inhabit our space.

The message of the land might be that many forms of the expression of spirituality are right for these times. The lessons of the natural world, which thrives with conifers and broadleaf trees, with a thousand molluscs, crustaceans, fish and mammals in the deep sea and myriad species of flora and fauna, from fungus to mighty elk, all co-existing and involved in symbiotic relationships, is that diversity is essential to health and that there is room for all.

Our truth does not have to be *the* truth, to be judged against others; just as we do not have to judge the respective worth of the oak and the thorn; we need both. Tuning into the land, the myriad expressions of differing life needed for the health of the planet help us recognise that choice and diversity are good and necessary to keep our earth and ourselves in good heart. All that we need to do then is to respect other faiths and spiritualities and address ourselves to our own journey, and how we can be of service as a part of it.

So let us pause one last time, for the sunset is calling us once again. As our mind's eye leads us to the hill that overlooks the lake reflecting the sun's glorious descent, consider for a moment – why the sunset?

Why not dawn, midday or deep midnight, which are also liminal times? Perhaps because a certain wistfulness seems to be written into the DNA of the Celts; it is expressed in an untranslatable Welsh word, *hiraeth* – homesickness, longing, nostalgia. The Celtic folk soul yearns to the west, the place of sunset and of the sea that leads to the paradisal isles and the magical orchards of the ever-young, where bud, flower and fruit can be found simultaneously on the trees, perfuming the air. Perhaps the longing is common to all of us, and the reason that we seem fully to value things only when we realise their finite nature.

But now, in this evening of our imagination, the flaming sky reminds us that there is also an inner fire within us, just as the sun is reflected in the earth's fiery core, connecting us to the source of physical life as we know it: as within, so without.

Duplicating our physical connection with the world, of touch, smell, hearing, smelling, seeing, we have, deep within, a connective and loving heart that beats in rhythm with our ancestors, our landscape; as within, so without.

Shall we reach out to the landscape or surrender to what is within? This is not a choice that we have to make. At any time we can be present in two worlds, fully engaged in the everyday, yet with an awareness of union, of our place on the magical web of life, shaken by its least quiver and responding intuitively to each. To bring the gifts and wisdom of the past and the natural world into our present is to connect to the spirit of Druidry. To develop this awareness to inform our every action is the true gift of the ancestral heart. Without it, life is simply existence; but once gained, the universe and the ages of man, the magic of relationship with the whole of life, the realm of the Gods as expressed through the kingdom of nature, is spread out before us.

Bibliography

Harvey, G. 2005. *Animism: Respecting the Living World*. Hurst & Company, London.

Matthews, John (ed.) 1999. *The Bardic Source Book*, Blandford Press, London.

Afterword

By Ronald Hutton

It is a privilege and an honour to be asked to comment on this collection of essays. At first sight I may not be the most appropriate person to do so, as I am very much an insider to the world portrayed within it. Although a few of the contributors – who include some whom I have most enjoyed – were not formerly known to me, I am acquainted with most, by reputation or (much more frequently) in person. Several are friends, and I have provided references to assist the careers of some and been an active collaborator in the spiritual journeys that some describe in these pages. For example, I was present in the sweat lodge that provided the launch-point for the relationship of one with his wolf-spirit, and at the Gorsedd ceremony at Avebury that marked another nodal point in it, and myself cooked the venison feast that precipitated another. Part of my pleasure in reading the successive chapters, indeed, has been that they have enabled me to get to know people of whom I am already fond still better: my all-time favourite moment in doing so was to experience Robert Wallis's lovely home and homeland through his own eyes. At other times, such as in the case of Luzie Wingen's gem of an introduction to genetics, I was provided with an enhanced understanding of a field that was less well known to me.

It is precisely because the collection does its work so well, and represents such a fine summary of a set of inter-related world pictures, that I feel emboldened to ask a series of searching questions about those. If it sums up a cluster of attitudes and ideologies to such effect, perhaps we can now go on to probe more deeply into those, and see if they can be expressed yet more effectively, and loose ends in them tied and possible gaps in them plugged. If this is the case, then perhaps what is represented here can be made still more readily communicable, and have a still broader application and relevance to the current social, environmental and ethical problems. These essays deal, between them, with two closely related phenomena: the natural world and the ancestors, and I shall treat each in turn.

First of all, what is nature? The most obvious and superficial answers to that question will depend greatly on where in the Western world one lives. In large areas of North America, and some parts of northern and eastern Europe, it means a genuine wilderness, into which humans make varying kinds of intervention. In much of Europe, however, and especially Britain, it usually means the countryside, a series of landscapes manufactured by our species over thousands of years: by the Neolithic, at latest, we were making wholesale transformations of large areas from a natural to an artificial environment, for our own benefit. Did 'nature', in the sense of basic biological engineering, intend us to remain on the African savannah, to which we are physically adapted? Or is it 'natural', in the sense of an inherent outcome of evolution, for us to behave inventively and imperiously, to colonise the whole terrestrial globe, and interfere with every ecosystem into which we enter? How can we be at once part of nature, if everything is connected, and yet outside it?

Come to think of it, what does this language of interconnection actually mean, if we are operating in an environment our own kind has manipulated and worked over for so long? Are we in charge of the connections, and are they maintained by our own daily efforts? If not, who or what is in charge, and where do we fit in? If so, how does this relate to a language of inherently – even divinely – constructed connection, our place in which needs to be understood afresh? If it is 'natural' to us to tune in to all that is sacred, whole and inviolable, why do those who advocate such a position also emphasise that strenuous daily spiritual effort is needed to do it? Furthermore, where are the limits to such reconnection, such sanctity, and such wholeness? We can clearly feel ourselves (if we wish) to be one with the wolf and other charismatic fauna, with trees and with flowers; but are we equally as one with lethal, crippling or disfiguring viruses, bacilli and bacteria, and with the rat, the tapeworm, the louse, the skin fungus, the slug and the clothes moth? Has not our entire existence, since our species evolved, been bound up with partnering or commandeering many aspects of nature while combating many others, even seeking their annihilation if possible? When we weed our flower beds or mow our lawns, are these actions examples of reverence, reconnection and holistic living, or are they something else? Also, how do these questions relate to that of an inherent sanctity in the natural world? If everything in it is sacred, than how can there be any particular sacred sites? If, as many indigenous peoples certainly believe, not only all animate beings and all places but also inanimate objects, such as stoves and tools, have indwelling spirits, what distinguishes a pot or a flint on a museum shelf from a human bone that suggests that any of those objects should be given special treatment?

All this refers to the apparent world, but many of the contributors to this volume are very conscious of another, which is traditionally and loosely referred to as that of spirits; a term I shall retain here. Traditional peoples certainly often make no fast boundaries between physically apparent animals and trees, and the invisible but active and often very potent and interfering entities that have been known for hundreds of years, in Latin-influenced languages, as spirits: which is why the newly fashionable expression 'other than human beings', taken from one anthropologist in his study of a Native American people, serves to cover all. Even traditional peoples, however, who included all Europeans until modern times, recognise that most individuals cannot see or hear spirits, which is why most, if not all, such peoples have had specialists who are expert in dealing with them. Modern societies have generally concluded that there is no objective evidence for the existence of them, and collectively regard themselves as getting along perfectly well without dealings with them, or the recognition of the need for any. At the same time they also generally recognise that a personal belief in them, like one in deities, is a legitimate private matter, as are personal techniques to deal with them. Does this situation pose any problem for those who believe in nature spirits, ancestral spirits and related kinds of entity in the modern age? Does it set them free to practice, and to offer their skills and understanding to others without fear of persecution? Or is there something inherently flawed and menacing in the de-spiritualised condition of modern society, which needs to be resisted and remedied? If so, why, and by whom, and with what right?

With that last discussion, I have already begun to encroach on the theme of 'the ancestors', and it is worth starting a discussion of that with the observation that the sense in which the expression is used in this collection is neither that of our own society nor that of traditional societies elsewhere in the world. In English, our ancestors have usually been understood as forebears in our own bloodline. In societies elsewhere in which human ancestors are regarded as a vital component of communal spirituality – which are a minority among human communities as a whole – they are understood in a different sense. There they function as a collective force that intervenes constantly and potently in the affairs of the living. If dealt with properly they can confer good fortune and health, but if neglected or offended, they send affliction and disaster; in that sense they play the same part in those cultures as nature spirits, deities and/or human magicians do in others. The ancestors who feature in this collection seem to be collective entities like those of traditional peoples, but considerably less interventionist, imperious and menacing. So where have they come from, and how do they fit into anybody's tradition?

They also seem to be both ancient and amorphous, and to

grow more all-knowing and powerful the older they are. So where, exactly, are they: in our world, in a parallel one, or a next one? How does this cosmology fit in with one of interconnection and of rebirth, reincarnation and transmigration, if they are indeed unchanging and immortal human personalities with whom we can make contact? Why is it, also, that more recent spiritual ancestors seem to get neglected, in favour of those who are ancient enough to lack faces, names and individual traits, unless we invent or dream those for ourselves? The case of Druidry may stand here as an exemplar of this question. There are plenty of examples of people who called themselves Druids in the past three hundred years who can justly be admired and recalled by those who use the name today, for their courage, creativity and political and cultural radicalism. They tend, however, usually to get by-passed in favour of the 'original', ancient Druids. At first sight this may seem natural – as a going back to the fount of inspiration – but the ancient Druids are not only mysterious, they are mute, at least in any objective, apparent and collectively accessible sense. What we have of them are a few images produced and repeated by ancient foreigners (often enemies), which may all be projected fantasies onto which we are now projecting our own. Are we honouring the Iron Age Druids by doing so, or just engaging in another round of exploitation? In the wider sense, most contributors to this book stand in a line of historic writers who have advocated a greater communion with nature, a spirit world and/or a more admirable past, ever since urbanisation, industrialisation and a celebration of progress began. Why are these undoubted and identifiable spiritual ancestors not celebrated more often in books such as this?

Can it be that the nameless, faceless, mysterious prehistoric dead are a more convenient focus for memorialisation and eulogy as ancestors because they are more malleable? Or, do we feel that too few other people try to speak for them, and that they are more exploited and objectified in general than the historic dead?

If the latter idea has some truth in it, then there may be a further irony: that advances in technology enable us to know ancient people better than ever before. We can now reconstruct their living faces, and know what they ate, in which terrain they grew up, what health they enjoyed (or suffered), how they lived, and how they farmed and used crafts. We can reconstruct their environment with ever greater clarity, both the nature of their 'natural' landscape and the human-made structures that they erected within it. None of these advances, however, have demonstrably been achieved by mystical communion. They are all the work of scientists and technicians working in partnership with archaeologists and heritage managers, the most obvious and effective current communicators with and guardians of our ancient predecessors. So what should or could be done to make a relationship between them, and more overtly spiritualised approaches to prehistory, more directly complementary?

Finally, one of the lessons of archaeology is that our ancestors, through the ages, have done everything needed to prepare the way for our modern lifestyles. Since our species first entered Europe, it has struggled to combat cold, hunger, disease, injury, harmful ignorance, boredom, early death and technological limitations. In the past couple of hundred years, tremendous advances have been made in all those enterprises, with clear benefits for humanity. The collateral damage and overkill produced in the process is now obvious to all, while the solutions to much of it are not. Why, then, should we equate our ancestors, who prepared the way for these achievements and disasters, with traditional peoples elsewhere in the world who chose a different course? If we cannot find a positive answer to that question, why should we regard them as more wise and admirable than our forebears in the more recent past, or ourselves? Furthermore, do we not use the ideas and images that we take from them in different ways? The image of the wolf, across the Eurasian ancient world, was utilised most often by societies of violent young men, training to be raiders and warriors: as one of the essays here makes clear. Can we find a new use for what they represented, or can we make the wolf (and other large predators) represent something else in the collective imagination? Should there or could there even be such a thing as a collective imagination now?

Some of the contributors to this collection will justly feel that none of these questions apply to them, and a few will as justly feel that they have themselves recognised some of the issues concerned. Others may feel aggrieved, but they should not, if they really intend this book to have some effect on readers who are not already familiar with the ideas in it and merely seeking some further reassuring restatement of them. Those ideas have more relevance than individual emotional and recreational satisfaction, as Caitlín's reminder of their use in healing alone serves to prove. They do, however, currently serve mainly to define a particular post-hippy sub-culture, numerically quite large, but as yet a small minority in society at large, and to some extent at odds with it, consisting largely of well-educated, middle-class people in middle or old age. Back in 1974, in his best-seller *The Country and the City*, reflecting on the vogue for veneration of the countryside and of traditional lifestyles among the British, Raymond Williams grumbled about the way 'it suited the middle class to consider rural life a 'lost world'', so that 'the real land and its people were falsified'. His challenge has not yet really been answered, and it is time that it was met head-on, by facing up to such accusations and defeating them. This collection of essays shows how well a language of communion with the natural world and ancient peoples can still be expressed in the current time. If we can go on to work through the issues I have raised here, then we stand a very good chance of using our beliefs to make a real impact on society at large.

Biographies

Penny Billinton

Penny Billington is a Druid author, speaker, and celebrant who has been involved in the initiatives of the Order of Bards, Ovates and Druids for 20 years, and has edited the Order's journal 'Touchstone' for 14 years. She regularly leads workshops and retreats. Her published work includes *The Path of Druidry* (Llewellyn) a guide and comprehensive study course in Druidry, and a series of four novels starring a Druid detective who rights imbalances in the natural and mythic worlds. Her most recent book; *The Wisdom of Birch, Oak and Yew*, was published by Llewellyn in April 2015.

Jenny Blain

Former Senior Lecturer in Sociology, Sheffield Hallam University (recently retired), Dr Jenny Blain, originally from Scotland, has lived and worked as a lecturer in Canada and the UK. In addition to her book *Nine Worlds of Seid-Magic* (Routledge 2002) she has been editor with Graham Harvey and Doug Ezzy of *Researching Paganisms* (Altamira 2004), author with R J Wallis of *Sacred Sites, Contested Rites/Rights* (Sussex Academic Press, 2007) and numerous academic articles and chapters on Paganisms, Seidr, Heathenry, landscapes, ancestors and wights, and lately on Scottish identities. Having recently taken retirement she has returned to Scotland, where she is revising her earlier small book *Wights and Ancestors* and preparing a larger volume for Heathen practitioners provisionally titled *The Wyrd of the North*, in addition to her work as a genealogist helping others uncover their Scottish ancestries. She writes an occasional blog at http://landscapeself.blogspot.co.uk, which includes thoughts on place, politics, poetry and people.

Paul Davies

After attending several free festivals, campaigning against nuclear weapons and the NSA at Menwith Hill Peace Camp, North Yorkshire, Oddie (aka Paul) read Archaeological Theory and Social Anthropology at University of Wales, Lampeter, and went on to complete an MA in the Anthropology of Religion at the University of Durham. Oddie worked alongside many other people to bring the issue of ancestry, and specifically the reburial of human remains, into the public domain. He is a Quaker, absolute pacifist and independent Druid of several groups including the Bards of Caer Abiri, OBOD and is an associate member of the BDO.

Camelia Elias

Camelia Elias is Associate Professor of American Studies, University of Roskilde, Denmark.

Greywolf

Greywolf (aka Philip Shallcrass) has been a Druid since 1974 and is currently chief of the British Druid Order. He is a writer, musician, singer-songwriter, artist, drum-maker, roundhouse-builder and thatcher. Greywolf and Bobcat were the first to raise the issue of respectful reburial for ancient human remains unearthed in Britain. Greywolf lives in rural Wiltshire with two of his three sons. For more information, visit the BDO website at druidry.co.uk and Greywolf's blog at greywolf.druidry.co.uk. The BDO offers distance learning courses in Druidry and Philip is the author of *Druidry: A Practical and Inspirational Guide* and *A Druid Ogham Oracle*. Greywolf also co-authored *A Druid Directory* with Bobcat.

Graham Harvey

Graham Harvey is Professor of Religious Studies at the Open University, President of the British Association for the Study of

Religion, and widely known for research about animism among indigenous and other communities. His research and publications largely engage with Jews, Pagans and indigenous peoples and often focus on ritual and etiquette in human relationships with the larger-than-human world.

Sarah Hollingham

Sarah Hollingham is a Chartered Water and Environment Manager working for the Environment Agency. Sarah has been attending Quaker meetings for about 23 years and lives by the sea in Suffolk with her two children and lots of maps. Her publications include *Marine Aggregate Dredging: A Review of Current Procedures for Assessing Coastal Processes and Impact at the Coastline* and *Using Feature Films in Geography Teaching.*

Ronald Hutton

Ronald is Professor of History at The University of Bristol, a leading authority on history of the British Isles in the sixteenth and seventeenth centuries, on ancient and medieval Paganism and magic, and on the global context of witchcraft beliefs; also probably the leading historian of the ritual year in Britain and of modern Paganism.

David Loxley

Chief Druid of the Druid Order since 1981 and a member since 1970. www.thedruidorder.org

Caitlín Matthews

Caitlín Matthews is the author of over 65 books including *Singing the Soul Back Home* and *Celtic Visions*. She is co-founder of FíOS, the Foundation for Inspirational and Oracular Studies, dedicated to the sacred and unwritten arts. She teaches shamanic and ancestral courses internationally, and has a shamanic healing practice in Oxford dealing with soul-sickness and ancestral fragmentation. www.hallowquest.org.uk

Emma Restall Orr

Emma (aka Bobcat) spent 25 years studying and working within Druidry, as a tutor in The Order of Bards Ovates and Druids, as joint chief in The British Druid Order, and then founded The Druid Network. Bobcat and Greywolf were the first to raise the issue of respectful reburial for ancient human remains unearthed in Britain. In 2004, Emma founded Honouring the Ancient Dead, an advocacy group working for the respectful treatment of ancestral material. In 2006 she opened a natural burial ground and nature reserve in the heart of England where she lives with her husband. Emma is the author of many books including; *Living With Honour: A Pagan Ethics* and *The Wakeful World: Animism, Mind and the Self in Nature*.

Robert Wallis

Robert J Wallis has written extensively on the archaeology and anthropology of art, and the re-presentation of the past in the present by contemporary Pagans and neo-Shamans. Wallis is currently working on a monograph critically examining the interface between *Art and Shamanism: From Cave Painting to the White Cube*, a co-edited book on *Archaeologists, Pagans and Ancestors*, a revised and expanded edition of the co-authored *Historical Dictionary of Shamanism*, and the ten-year anniversary edition of the co-authored *Galdrbok: Practical Heathen Runecraft, Shamanism and Magic*. He is a keen falconer and plans to become similarly passionate about bee-keeping.

Luzie Wingen

Norwich Quaker and Quantitative Geneticist at the John Innes Centre.

Endnotes

Tribes of Spirit: Animals as Ancestors *by Greywolf*

1. www.youtube.com/watch?v=gFF0X7EZXxo accessed 21/11/14
2. www.heorot.dk/dramatis.html# accessed 18/02/2015
3. Title track from a forthcoming CD

Ancestors and Place: Seidr and Other Ways of Knowing *by Jenny Blain*

1. Indeed Tolley (2009) takes the account of the Greenland seeress to be purely a Christian fiction, with the seeress Þorbjörg as a sort of anti-bishop. Without going into details here, I don't agree, but consider that while the story is told to further the importance of Guðríðr (who became an ancestor of many leading Icelanders) it also holds echoes of practices that may have persisted into the early years of Christianity, or even beyond and hence into the memories of the listeners who heard the saga recited.

2. Or in my translation:
   Etins I mind, eldest born
   Those who earliest did me raise,
   Nine worlds I mind, nine etin women.

Healing the Ancestral Communion: Pilgrimage Beyond Time and Space *by Caitlín Matthews*

1. www.shakespeareswords.com/cousin

Memory at Sites of Non-Place: A Eulogy *by Camelia Elias*

1. In *Measure for Measure*, Isabella says to Angelo: 'Go to your bosom; Knock there, and ask your heart what it doth know,' suggesting that there's yet another language we can all speak.
2. Courtesy of collector K. Frank Jensen, who was also a member

of the organisation, and who kindly gave me permission to photograph some of this material.

3. Obituary by Ashphodel P. Long 1986: 'Colin Murray – In Memoriam' in *Wood and Water*, 20. Winter Solstice.

Index

Moon Books invites you to begin or deepen your encounter with Paganism, in all its rich, creative, flourishing forms.